ERTSON
JOHN'S
TO LET

John Kay
OF EDINBURGH

Barber, miniaturist and social commentator

1742–1826

JOHN KAY
(*Self portrait in oils*)

Courtesy of the Scottish National Portrait Gallery

John Kay

OF EDINBURGH

Barber, miniaturist and social commentator

1742 – 1826

HILARY AND MARY EVANS

IMPULSE PUBLICATIONS

ABERDEEN 1973

First published 1973 by
Impulse Publications Limited,
28 Guild Street, Aberdeen

SBN 901311 28 6

Printed in Great Britain by
J. W. Arrowsmith Ltd., Bristol

Contents

Acknowledgements

The authors' thanks are due to the staffs of the following establishments: The Edinburgh Public Libraries, particularly Mrs. Armstrong of the Edinburgh Room; the Royal Scottish Academy; the Scottish National Portrait Gallery; the National Gallery of Scotland, Department of Prints & Drawings; and the Huntly House Museum, Edinburgh. Also to Neil Rhind and George Suckling for their interest and encouragement; and above all to Paul Harris, our publisher, who has personally identified himself with the Quest for Kay at every stage.

1

The Quest for Kay

The only place in his native Edinburgh where any of John Kay's works are on public show is at the handsome 'Kenilworth' public house in Rose Street. Here, if you visit the toilets, you will find that the customary isometric 'Gent' and 'Lady' have been replaced by Kay figures of the appropriate sexes.

Otherwise, Kay's work must be hunted for. The Scottish National Portrait Gallery possesses the portrait which we reproduce as our frontispiece, but it was not on public display at the time of our last visit. None of his works are on exhibition at the National Gallery or any other of the city's museums, though most possess some of his work and will willingly show it to visitors. Several of those we spoke to in the course of our quest were a little vague as to who exactly we were talking about; and of those who did know of him, few had any great opinion of his work and most found our enthusiasm hard to understand.

Such an attitude on the part of the Establishment, coupled with the century and more of almost complete neglect which has shadowed Kay and his work, might have been discouraging, were it not that the majority of private people to whom we have introduced him have been enthusiastic. Is it a question of a prophet failing to be honoured in his own country? Or is it simply the wheel of fashion, which is finally bringing his work back into favour after so prolonged a neglect?

One significant indication that attitudes are in fact changing is afforded by the rise in prices which sets of Kay's etchings have been fetching in the saleroom over the past quarter-century. In 1948 you might have picked one up for as little as £1: the highest recorded price paid up to 1962 was £16. Today, though no doubt you might still hope to find a copy at a bargain price, you could count yourself lucky to find a set under £30; and it is certain that prices will rise even more steeply in the immediate future.

Those who know Kay's work are apt to feel about him as if he was a personal discovery. In the first place, they are unlikely to have come across a reference to him in the art histories, and even less likely to have seen examples of his work reproduced even in surveys devoted to graphic art. It is rare to find his name mentioned, rarer still to read a word of appreciation of his talent. So when by some happy accident they stumble across his work, it is liable to strike with a freshness of impact not often experienced in this over-communicative age when our senses are apt to be numbed by over-exposure to the world's 'art treasures'.

Having made that first traumatic discovery, the discoverer of Kay begins to realise that he has found his way into a secret and very personal world. At first sight it seems a real enough world, populated by identifiable historical personages – Adam Smith the economist, Tom Paine the revolutionary, Sir Walter

Scott the novelist, Vincent Lunardi the balloonist. Yet at the same time it is a world of fancy, where these true-life figures are transformed into characters in a private pageant. Chosen by the artist for their separate and varied personalities, all alike come to share a magical unreality as a result of being presented to us through his unique and individual vision.

If Kay has suffered from continuous official neglect, this can be blamed in part on his own skill. His work happens to comprise a gallery of portraits almost unique in history – several hundred likenesses of men and women from all walks of life who composed Edinburgh society at the turn of the eighteenth and nineteenth centuries. As documents, his prints are clearly of unique value: as works of art, their appeal is less immediately obvious. Consequently, where they have been valued at all, it has been as documentation.

Of course they do indeed possess their inestimable documentary value. But to stop there is to miss a remarkable personal vision of the way people – not just individual historical personages, but people simply as people – look and move and act. And incidentally, to overlook a very individual artistic experience.

For the authors of this book, the quest of Kay has been an exciting and rewarding pursuit. The more we learnt about the man and his work, the more indignant we came to feel at the way he has been passed over by history, the more determined we became to do what we could to win him back the recognition he deserves. We trust that this book is only the first step. Without doubt, there must be a great deal more of his work to be identified and located. Where, for instance, are all the miniatures which formed the staple of his daily work, which earned the bread that fed him and his family? Most must have been purchased by their sitters, and even now are probably in private hands throughout Scotland and perhaps dispersed even farther afield, unrecognised and probably little valued.

Again, there must be more water-colours, for those we found showed that he had some degree of expertise in this medium. And there must be other oil-paintings besides the self-portrait we reproduce as our frontispiece, for it is hardly credible that an artist should execute only a single work in a medium. Besides, in the other self-portrait we reproduce as plate iii, Kay depicts himself as painting, in oils, what seems to be a meeting of some fraternity – the Guild of Barber-Surgeons, perhaps, of which he was a member; or his Masonic Lodge; or simply a gathering of friends at some friendly tavern. Where is that painting now?

As for the self-portrait itself, we discovered it in an unlabelled folio volume on the lowest shelf of a basement bookcase in the Royal Scottish Academy, where it gave every appearance of having sat undisturbed for decades at least.

Doubtless we should be grateful that it has survived at all – such fugitive items could so easily have been lost or destroyed when the artist or his widow died. But once having been rescued, it is to be feared they owe their further preservation to the fact that they were *not* valued; that priceless volume of Kay's sketches and early prints has survived intact precisely because nobody cared very much what happened to it.

So the neglect into which Kay and his work have fallen has its beneficial side; nevertheless on balance we must have lost more than we have gained. When we first approached one of the few known possessors of Kay's work, they denied owning anything; only when we found a further strong indication that they did indeed possess some material, and persisted politely but as firmly as we could, was the

iii Self-portrait at easel, watercolour

material unearthed. It is reproduced in our pages for the first time. Again, the remarkable picture which forms our endpapers exists in one form or another in three of Edinburgh's museums; yet it was apparent to us that not all those who possess it were aware that the figures were 'borrowed' from Kay, any more than the author of the history-book in which we first found it reproduced simply as 'an old print'. True, neither the painters nor the engravers saw fit to acknowledge their debt, and Kay's name appears nowhere either on the picture-frame or on the engraved print. None the less, today when standards of morality in art are somewhat higher than they were, one would have hoped that justice would be done and credit given where it was due.

And this, ultimately, is the purpose of the present book: to prevent any further loss of the scanty remaining Kay material, and to give what does remain the recognition it deserves. We found enough in the course of our quest to add a good deal to the available information about Kay. To most of those who know him at all, he is simply the strange ex-barber who drew the *Original Portraits*, and indeed they are his principal legacy and will always remain so. But we trust the pages which follow will show that there is considerably more to Kay than that, and possibly awaken art historians to the fact that his artistic talents are not so negligible as they have been considered hitherto.

The scope of Kay's art is admittedly limited; but what he did, he did better than anyone anywhere. He was a perceptive chronicler of his times – but that does not mean his work must be relegated to the illustration of history books. He was a citizen of Edinburgh who depicted other citizens of Edinburgh – but that does not mean his art is unintelligible outside Scotland. His pictures are full of humour – but that does not mean they cannot be taken seriously as art. Recognition of Kay's unique talent is long overdue: it is high time he was admitted to his rightful place among the ranks of the world's truly original graphic artists.

2

John Kay's Edinburgh

John Kay's pictures are of their place and of their time. The city he lived in, the community he lived among, had their own very individual character, they made his art possible, and influenced what he did and how he did it.

To understand Kay's Edinburgh, we must first come to terms with its size. The population of the city when he first set up in business was around 60,000 – that is, it was not much larger than Kilmarnock today, or Hastings or Harrogate. By the end of his life the population had passed the 100,000 mark, but this still left it a relatively small place compared with the modern city.

Yet Edinburgh was, after all, the second city of Britain and the capital of a great nation which still, notwithstanding the Act of Union of 1707, preserved a considerable degree of independence. Its streets had seen a capital city's share of the violence, bloodshed and dispute, relieved by occasional moments of glory, which sadly make up the pages of history. Less than London, but more than any other city of Britain, Edinburgh had its own entity and character distinct from – and often opposed to – the country surrounding it.

The physical aspect of Edinburgh in Kay's time is effectively described in Cook's *Universal British Traveller* of 1779, published while the artist was still working as a barber:

> This ancient and opulent city possesses a boldness and grandeur of situation not to be conceived. It is built on the edges and sides of a vast sloping rock, of a great and precipitous height at the upper extremity, and the sides declining very quick and steep into a plain. The view of the houses at a distance strikes the traveller with wonder; their own loftiness, improved by their almost aerial situation, gives them a look of magnificence not to be found in any other part of Great Britain. All these conspicuous buildings, which form the upper part of the city, are of stone, and make a handsome appearance; they are in general six or seven storeys high in front; but by reason of the declivity of the hill much higher backward; one in particular, called Babel, has about twelve or thirteen storeys.

The distant view of Edinburgh might strike the approaching traveller with wonder, but even from afar off he might suspect that Edinburgh had its drawbacks:

> 'This, then, is Edinburgh?' said the youth (in Sir Walter Scott's *The Abbot*), as the fellow travellers arrived at one of the heights to the southwards, which commanded a view of the great northern capital, 'This is that Edinburgh of which we have heard so much?'
>
> 'Even so,' said the falconer, 'yonder stands Auld Reekie – you may see the smoke hang over her at twenty miles distance, as the goss-hawk hangs over a plump of young wild-duck.'

And when the traveller reached his destination he might well be further dismayed, like 24-year-old Edward Topham, visiting Edinburgh in 1774:

> A person like you, who has always been accustomed to meet with downy pillows and splendid apartments in the hotels of Paris and Lyons, can scarcely form in imagination the distress of a miserable stranger on his first entrance into this city, as there is no inn that is better than an alehouse, nor any accomodation that is decent, cleanly or fit to receive a gentleman. We were conducted by a poor devil of a girl without shoes or stockings, and with only a single linsey-woolsey petticoat which just reached halfway to her ankles, into a room where about twenty Scotch

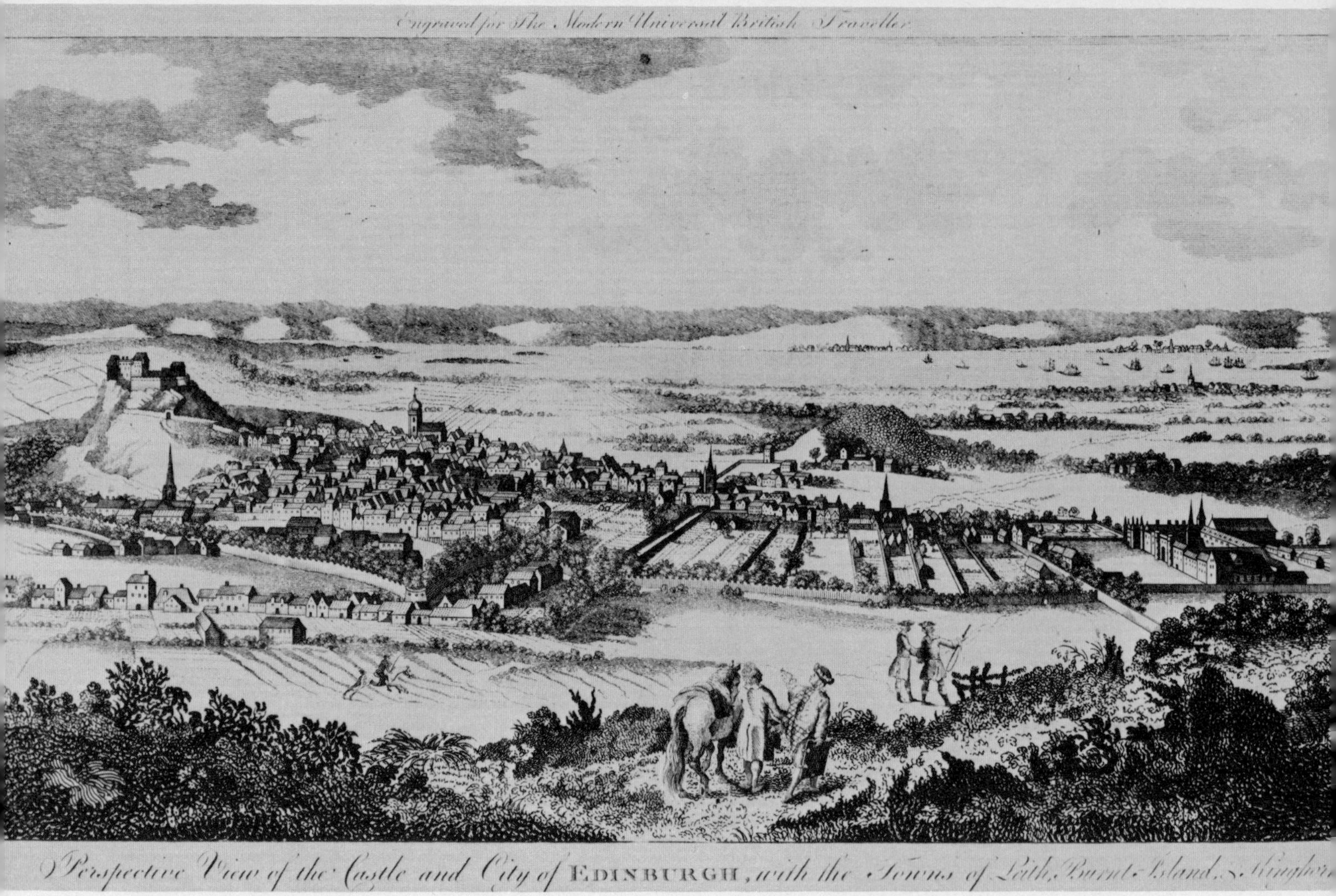
Engraved for The Modern Universal British Traveller
Perspective View of the Castle and City of EDINBURGH, with the Towns of Leith, Burnt Island, & Kinghorn

iv Edinburgh in 1779

drovers had been regaling themselves with whisky and potatoes. You may guess our amazement when we were informed that this was the best inn in the metropolis.

The poverty of Scotland in the early eighteenth century has been vividly described by Henry Grey Graham in his great book *The Social Life of Scotland in the Eighteenth Century*. Compared with England, Scotland was wretchedly poor – poor in wealth and poor in spirit. The Act of Union, the disasters of 1715 and 1745, had – quite understandably – induced a state of apathy from which a lesser race might never have recovered. The wonder is not that the Scots remained in stupor for half a century, but that they ever managed to snap out of it at all.

The filth of Edinburgh was so notorious that Richard Twiss, travelling in Spain in 1772, used it as a yardstick, commenting that 'Madrid, some years ago, might have vied with Edinburgh in filthiness'. At ten each evening, sensitive households started to burn

v Edinburgh High Street in the early nineteenth century

brown paper; for this was the hour when slops – known as 'the Flowers of Edinburgh' – were emptied from the high windows onto the cobbles below, there to lie all night before collection (and all day too on Sunday, when street cleaning was considered impious).

However, conditions were improving during Kay's lifetime: the city magistrates began to enforce stricter laws, and the passer-by who received a pail of slops over his head had at least some legal recourse. This trivial detail is one sign of how pride was beginning to ebb back; more significantly, this was the time when Edinburgh started to expand beyond its old confines, spreading beyond the North Loch to lay the foundations of the handsome New Town which is the outward symbol of that astonishing renaissance which constitutes the golden age of the Modern Athens.

For Kay's Edinburgh was not only small, it was also remarkably compact. Our engraving of 1779 shows how the city was virtually confined to the area between the Castle on the West and the Canongate on the East: it embodied only a few streets of the modern city. Kay lived in the High Street and had his shop in Parliament Close which was virtually part of the same street.

It was in many ways still a medieval city in concept. Houses crowded one on another

vi Part of the Old Town, Edinburgh

with little regard for privacy or convenience. The towering 'lands', built of dark granite from the quarries of Cragleith, were impressive to view but inconvenient to live in – their inhabitants might have enlightened modern planners about some of the drawbacks of high-rise developments. Each land was really a vertical street. It had a common staircase, and each storey housed at least one separate household. A typical land might have menial labourers in the cellars, a noble lord, a merchant or a professional gentleman in the lower storeys, clerks and shopkeepers higher up, and in the garret, more working men. Certainly it was very democratic: inevitably, though, it was dark and confined: access to the street was inevitably tiresome and generally squalid into the bargain.

Such (comments Sir Herbert Maxwell) was the sordid environment for which the county fashionables were eager to exchange the fresh air of the hillside or coast in order to take part in the gaieties of the Edinburgh season. Of the houses they occupied many have been 'improved' away; those which remain excite our wonder that wealthy peers and refined women should be content with such quarters.

Here, nevertheless, the citizens of Edinburgh lived and worked at one another's elbows. Trades tended to congregate, again as in a medieval city; it was no accident that Kay set up in business in Parliament Close, for the locality was noted for booksellers as well as for silversmiths.

Day and night, the heart of Edinburgh was a crowded, busy place. The *Gentleman's Magazine* for May 1766 observes, 'So great a crowd of people are nowhere else confined in so small a space, which makes their streets as much crowded every day as others are at a fair.' It all tended to generate a tightly-knit, very public, way of life, more continental than

vii Fireman and linkboy

British: and the nature of most men's residences led to a further characteristic more associated with continental cities than British, the tendency to choose the tavern or the club as a meeting place, rather than invite friends and acquaintances back into the home. Thus the city provided the richest possible field for a talent like Kay's. He could see his subjects passing his house door or shop window almost daily; when he put up his prints in his window, they would recognise one another by sight if not by name. For this was a place, in Graham's phrase, 'where every face was known, and few domestic secrets were hid'.

A populace who had recovered their old self-confidence and pride: a community close-knit and intimate; such was the Edinburgh society among which Kay lived and worked. But there was a third factor, perhaps the most important of all: the intellectual climate of the place and the age.

Union with England had made Edinburgh nominally a provincial city, and provincial it might easily have become in fact. Inevitably, London exerted a pull which men of ambition found it hard to resist: there were careers to be made in the south for which Scotland offered no scope. We cannot blame poor

Boswell if he could find no ready response to Johnson's dig, that 'the noblest prospect which a Scotchman ever sees is the high road that leads him to England'. A good many Scots, like Boswell himself, were eager to take that road: it is significant that in 1760 there had been only a single stagecoach running each month between London and Edinburgh, and the journey took 15 days; by 1786 two coaches a *day* were leaving the Grassmarket, and the journey had been cut to as little as 60 hours.

Yet the road from Edinburgh to London was also the road from London to Edinburgh. What was happening was not that Scottish talent was migrating, rather that it was proving itself capable of playing a growing part in the affairs of the Union. Scotland at this period supplied the United Kingdom with many of its great men – its statesmen and its judges, its doctors and economists, its writers and inventors. They might take their ideas to market in London; but it was Edinburgh which fostered them and gave them the stimulus they needed.

Edinburgh had always been a place for men and women with ideas. In the previous century, those ideas had taken physical shape and come to blows one with another: Scotland had been so riven by religious and political disputes – and most often the two at once – that it had been named 'the Killing Time'. Now, whether through simple exhaustion, or the assertion of a more rational spirit, the people of Scotland, like those of London and (for the time being) Paris, were content to breathe the calm air of the Age of Reason. The intellectual climate of Kay's Edinburgh was one of balance, toleration and moderation – and it is reflected in every drawing he made.

The drink helped, no doubt. Every commentator on life in eighteenth century Edinburgh is forced to marvel at the quantity of drinking that went on. For many a respectable citizen, the day started with his 'morning' – a glass of ale or brandy: ale or claret washed down his breakfast: and the clock striking half-past-eleven gave him the signal for his 'meridian' – a further gill of ale: and so on, throughout the day. Claret was then the gentleman's preferred tipple: whisky was a Highland drink, for drovers and their kind. The Scots really loved their claret: the household of Forbes of Culloden got through £40 worth in a month, at a time when the top price was 18*s* a dozen – which makes some 20 bottles a day. Business deals were sealed in drink, lawyers discussed their briefs over drink, meeting an acquaintance in the street called for a drink, and so throughout the working day till evening came and no further excuses were needed, and toasts, healths and sentiments could follow in unsteady sequence till long after the town guard had beat the 10 o'clock tattoo up the High Street and down the Canongate.

Not, of course, that drink made the Scots let go their characteristic earnestness: but perhaps it helped them shed the acrimony that had formerly accompanied it. Whatever the cause, bigotry was losing some of its bitterness. When the Presbytery of Dalkeith tried to prosecute Dr Alexander Carlyle, minister of Inveresk and one of Kay's subjects, for attending the tragedy of *Douglas*, the church courts refused to back them up; and when Mrs Siddons appeared on the Edinburgh stage in 1784, the Church Assembly was forced to suspend sittings because there were not sufficient present to form a quorum.

It was the same with politics. The pathetic if picturesque attempt of Prince Charles Stuart had been largely a Highland affair; the citizens of Edinburgh played for the most part only a reluctant role in the matter, and were probably relieved when it was all over. There were still loyal Jacobites, of course, who at the dinner table would pledge 'the King over the Water' by passing their glasses over the water-jug, and romantic girls who sighed sentimentally for Bonnie Prince Charlie, now grown rather stout and drinking himself gently to death in Italy. But the cause was a lost one, and perhaps in their hearts even the supporters of the House of Stuart were glad of it. And anyway, life had to go on.

The life of Edinburgh did indeed go on apace during Kay's lifetime. Though the population of Scotland increased only 50 per cent during the century, the revenue was multiplied 50-fold. The city enlarged its boundaries. Handsome new buildings appeared. Life grew more gracious – a gentleman could now provide each of his guests with a drinking-glass, instead of causing the single tumbler to circulate from one guest to the next. While Kay lived, Edinburgh remained a place where most men knew their neighbours, where friends lived within walking distance of one another and could expect to meet almost daily. But it was a society in ferment, growing in intellectual reach as well as in numbers, adding to its store of ideas as quickly as it added to its material possessions.

Looking out into the High Street from his house or into Parliament Close from his shop, John Kay could see the whole panorama of this new Edinburgh society parade before him – judges on their way to court, soldiers on their way to the parade-ground, ladies on their way to the assembly dances, wits and savants on their way to the Edinburgh Society for Encouraging Art, Science and Industry – or to the tavern, preachers on their way to church or chapel, beggars on their way to fruitful corners, tradesfolk on their way to market – all the disparate elements which make up a rich and variegated mosaic of society. And no ordinary society, either. In Graham's words:

> In no other country, surely, did there exist such marked individuality of character. Each one might retain his or her peculiarity, his or her whim of mind, oddity of life, or fancy of dress, in country seat or city flat. This striking originality of nature was found alike in judge and laird and minister, and in their spouses. The country swarmed with 'originals' in every rank, in town and village.

It was almost as though the society created the artist.

3

John Kay's Life

'He cared for no employment except that of etching likenesses,' Kay's widow reported. John Kay was an example of that still unexplained phenomenon, the born artist. He does not seem to have inherited any artistic tradition from his forebears: he received no encouragement to go in for art until he had proved that he possessed a talent which he was determined to use. And when he had found his true vocation, he exercised it only in the one field for which he seemed to have been fitted by nature. So far as we know, he never felt an urge to try his hand at a battle scene, or a mythological allegory, or even a modest landscape. Instead, he spent the 40-odd years of his artistic career single-mindedly 'etching likenesses'.

This single-mindedness explains in part why so little has been recorded about his later career. Once he had found his line, he kept to it unswervingly. If we know so little about his life, it is because there *was* so little to it – beyond the making of pictures.

Of his earlier years we do know a certain amount, thanks to a brief sketch of his own life which he himself drew up in 1792, when he had the idea of publishing a selection of his etchings in book form. He gives us the basic facts: we learn that he was born in April 1742, in a small house known as Gibraltar, a little to the south of Dalkeith, a market town some 11 km south-east of Edinburgh. His father, John Kay, was a mason in Dalkeith, as were his two paternal uncles James and Norman. His mother, Helen Alexander, was said to be heiress to a number of tenement buildings in Edinburgh, but her son claimed that she had been tricked out of them by relatives.

The elder John Kay died in 1748, and the boy was sent at the age of six to live with cousins at Leith, a harbour on the Firth of Forth, now part of Edinburgh. Here, Kay later claimed, he was ill-treated, neglected, beaten and starved. As if that were not enough, he suffered three near-fatal accidents in Leith harbour, on one occasion being fished out of the water and presumed dead until a sailor accidentally trampled on his belly, 'which immediately excited a groan'. We gather that he was separated from the rest of his family: nothing more is known about them, except that he is said to have had a brother and several other relatives living in America. Certainly he was later to make etchings – including portraits of Jefferson and Tom Paine (Plate 70) – based on miniatures sent from America.

'About this time,' (to quote his own words), 'he gave strong proofs of an uncommon genius for drawing, by sketching men, horses, cattle, houses, &c, with chalk, charcoal, or pieces of burnt wood, for want of pencils and crayons. But under the government of his cousins, no propensity of this kind was either attended to or encouraged.'

Young Kay had intentions of following in his father's footsteps as a mason; but luckily

viii Self-portrait with cat

for him – as it was to turn out – his cousins preferred to apprentice him, at the age of 13 or so, to a Dalkeith barber named George Heriot. Here he learnt the barber's trade; and though to begin with his work was mere drudgery, he found it a welcome change from his childhood privations at the hand of his 'barbarous relations'.

When the six statutory years of his apprenticeship had been completed, Kay moved into central Edinburgh. Here he served as journeyman with various barbers for what he states to have been seven years, though by the calendar it would seem to have been nearer nine (from 1762 to 1771).

He celebrated the end of his apprenticeship by getting married, to a Lilly Steven, who bore him ten children, all of whom died young except the eldest, William. He can hardly have been born later than 1775, and probably much earlier, since Lilly died in 1785; yet Kay tells us the boy was named after his own patron, William Nisbet of Dirleton. This would imply that Kay had already made the acquaintance of his benefactor at this early date. William, whom we know to have been still living in 1792, was said to have inherited some of his father's talent, and etched a few plates, one of which we reproduce as Plate xv: two others are included in the Collection of John Kay's etchings, and their authorship does not seem to have previously been questioned: yet their style reveals an inferior talent to John Kay's, even apart from the fact that

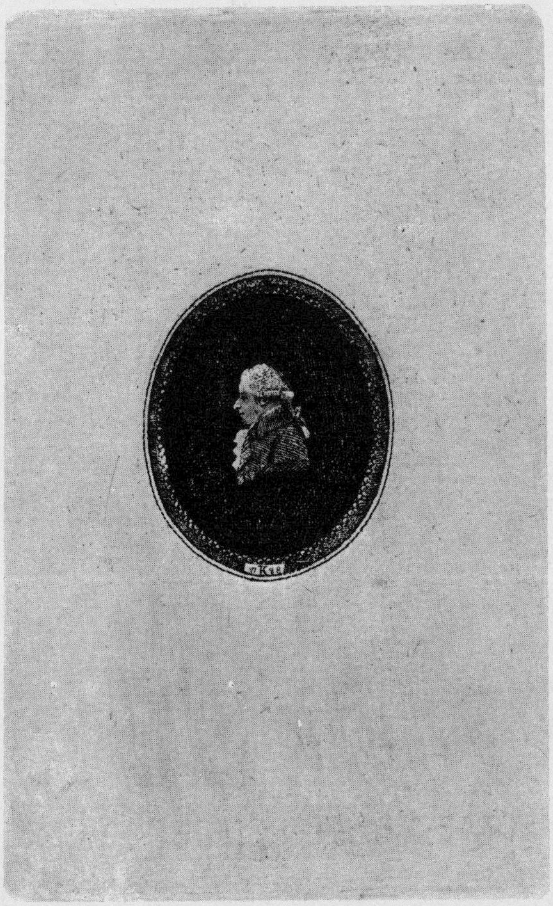

ix Self-portrait miniature

they are signed with a 'W'. (See notes to Plates xiv and xv.)

By 1771 the ambitious Kay was ready to set up in business as a barber on his own. Before he could do this, though, not being a native of Edinburgh, he had to obtain the freedom of the city. This he did on 19 December by purchasing it from the Society of Surgeon-Barbers, which cost him about £40.

The status of a barber at this period was considerably higher than we might expect. As Robert Chambers points out in his *Biographical Dictionary of Eminent Scotsmen*, 'The trade of a barber was then more lucrative, and consequently more dignified, than latterly. Kay had good employment in dressing the wigs and trimming the heads of a certain number of gentlemen every morning, all of whom paid him a certain annual sum (generally about 4 guineas) for his trouble.'

Kay carried on his business with considerable success for several years, and was employed by a number of the principal nobility and gentry in and about Edinburgh. Among these was a Mr William Nisbet, of Dirleton, near North Berwick, some 30 km from Edinburgh: he also had a town house in the Canongate, just down the road from Kay's shop. This gentleman, whom Chambers describes as 'a fine specimen of the old Jacobite country gentleman', was noted for his varied and cultivated tastes – he was a musician and even a

x Hamilton Bell's Wager: the print which the subject tried to get prohibited

composer on the one hand, and patronised gypsies on the other. He also patronised John Kay. Not only did he employ him professionally, but he took him on jaunts through the country in his carriage, invited him to stay at Dirleton, and (to quote Kay's own words again) 'at last became so fond of him, that for several years before he died, particularly the two last (1783–1784) he had him almost constantly with him, by night and by day'. This naturally interfered with the barbering business: fortunately Mr Nisbet was considerate enough to send regular sums of money to Mrs Kay as compensation for depriving her of her husband and his income.

Nisbet's patronage gave Kay leisure to work at his art. Encouraged by his benefactor, he executed many miniatures during this period, largely of the Nisbet family. His patron also promised to remember Kay in his will, but he kept putting off making the necessary arrangements, and when he died in 1784 no provision had been made. However, his heir was good enough to voluntarily settle an annuity of £20 on the artist, which was regularly paid for the rest of his life. In those days, such a sum was

xi The artist under examination: Kay (the central figure) defending himself for producing the previous print

sufficient to make a real difference to his fortunes.

Later in that year 1784, Kay made his first etchings. So far as is known, the first was either that reproduced here as Plate 2, or another on the same subject. Being recognisable portraits of well-known citizens and Edinburgh characters, the prints naturally aroused interest, and this encouraged Kay to take his art more seriously – if 'serious' is the word.

In March 1785 his wife died. Perhaps it was this release from responsibility which encouraged him to give up his barbering trade altogether, and set up as a miniaturist and printmaker. From 1785 for the rest of his life, Kay was able to live in tolerable comfort on the proceeds of his art, helped out by that useful annuity. He had a small shop at number 10 Parliament Close, on the south side of the square, off the High Street behind St Giles. Here, the window filled with his latest productions was a noted centre of attraction for passers-by and idlers. Cooke's *Modern Universal Traveller* tells us that the greater part of the houses in Parliament Close were inhabited either by booksellers or by silversmiths. The buildings were destroyed by fire in November 1824, just two years before Kay's death: he

xii A scene in the Caricature Ware Room, Edinburgh, 1796

J Kay 1798
THE MODERN CAIN'S LAMENT
O Harrie whether shall I fly: I am this day A Murderer of thousands, Every one that finds me will count me his Enemy and Slay me.

xiii The Modern Cain's Lament: satire on Pitt

may well have given up the shop by this time, in any case it is certain he made his last etching two years previously.

In 1785 Kay was initiated as a Freemason, in the Lodge of Saint David, Edinburgh: it is interesting to note that the Lodge celebrated the 150th anniversary of his initiation on 28 November 1935. In 1787, after two years of widowhood, Kay married his second wife, Margaret Scott. They lived happily, though so far as is known they had no children. Margaret survived him, dying in November 1835. They lived at 227 High Street, where there is today a pawnbroking establishment, just some 100 m from his shop.

It seems clear that Kay could have made more money from his art than he did, had he been more willing to work at what his clients wanted, instead of what he wanted to draw. Graham (in *The Social life of Scotland in the Eighteenth century*) is outspoken on the subject of the artistic climate of Scotland at this time: 'That Art may grow it is necessary that there should be taste; that an artist may live it is necessary that there be patrons; but in order that there be patrons it is further necessary that there should be money. Unfortunately, Scotland lacked all these requisites – money, taste, and patrons. . . . Classic themes no laird would look at; mythological subjects

xiv The City Guard, an imitation of Kay's subject-matter and style

none could understand; besides, propriety would be shocked with anything nude, and orthodoxy horrified at anything pagan. Portraits, and portraits alone, of the dead or living, could attract a customer.' But Kay's widow observed, 'he would suddenly quit his lucrative employment in miniature-drawing, in order to commit some freak of his fancy to copper, from which, perhaps, no profit was to be hoped for'. Fortunately for posterity, those freaks of fancy have been preserved more carefully than the miniatures. As for what Kay was actually paid, we have it on record that for a portrait of Lord Provost Sir James Hunter Blair, he agreed to receive 1 guinea for the first impression, and thereafter

xv The evening walk, by Kay's son William

at the rate of half-a-guinea for a further dozen prints. Not exactly lavish.

Many of his more satirical prints were purchased only to be destroyed by angry victims. On at least one occasion he was 'cudgelled', and in 1792 he was actually prosecuted for a satirical print showing a pedestrian match – strangely enough, by the winner. He successfully defended himself (see Plates x and xi) and got his own back by publishing the print which depicted his victory. When we remember that Kay was at the height of his career when the infinitely more savage Gillray and Rowlandson were at the height of theirs, it seems hard to believe that his gentle good-humoured sketches could possibly have caused offence; and, indeed, such cases seem to have been very much the exception. However, Plate xii seems to refer to another such occurrence.

Chambers tells an anecdote which reveals something about the man and his attitude to his art: 'Once he was "trysted" with an exceedingly ill-looking man, much pimpled, who, to add to the distresses of the artist, came accompanied by a fair nymph to whom he was about to be married. Honest Kay did all he could in favour of this gentleman, so far as omitting the ravages of bacchanalianism could go; but still he could not satisfy his customer, who earnestly appealed to his inamorata as to the injustice which he conceived to be done to him, and the necessity of improving the likeness. Quite tired at length, the miniaturist exclaimed, with an execration, that "he would paint every plook in the puppy's face, would *that* please him?"'

In 1792 Kay had the idea of publishing a selection of his plates in book form, but unfortunately the project came to nothing, probably for financial reasons. The fact that he conceived such a project shows that he had attained a certain measure of popular success: the fact that the project had to be abandoned showed that his position was not yet a secure one. In 1800 he paid a visit to London, doing a portrait of the younger Pitt on the occasion: whether this was an isolated journey we do not know.

We have no explicit statement about Kay's views and opinions, and he is so tolerant and so wide in his scope that there is little to be learnt even when we search his prints for internal evidence. But there is one aspect of his work which does seem significant, and this is an indication of sympathy with 'left-wing' ideas, during the years immediately following the outbreak of the French Revolution. This was not a time of political apathy – how could it be? – and until it became clear how the initial Republican spirit was being distorted into internecine feuds and the Napoleonic tyranny, there was much in the spirit of Revolutionary France to attract the liberal-minded foreigner. Scotland had its share of would-be reformers – and inevitably, of reactionary governors and judges. Kay's portraits at this time include many of these liberals – men such as Andrew M'Kinlay, David Downie, George Mealmaker and Robert Watt (his portrait was used as a frontispiece to *The Life and Character of Robert Watt*, published after the latter's execution). As for his engraving of the persecuted Thomas Muir, it includes the caption:

> Illustrious Martyr in the glorious cause
> Of truth, of freedom, and of equal laws.

Kay also depicted several known sympathisers with the French Republic, such as Thomas Hardy, Citizen M C Browne, Charles Sinclair (whose portrait is accompanied by the text 'Les privilèges finiront, mais le peuple est eternel' – a splendid sentiment for revolutionaries of all brands), Skirving ('A Tried Patriot and an Honest Man') and above all a genial portrait of Tom Paine, author of *The Rights of Man*, which was so popular that prints were being sold at 14 shillings apiece, a tidy sum for the period.

Is it too much to deduce from all this, that Kay himself had sympathy with the liberal cause? The suggestion is confirmed by the fact that these portraits are counterbalanced by three of Kay's rare excursions into straight political satire: an etching for William Wilkie's *Convention of Asses*, a satirical attack on the existing order of things: a satire on The Rev

Lapslie, one of Thomas Muir's accusers (see Plate 40); and the *Modern Cain's Lament*, lampooning Pitt's assumption of hostilities against the French Republic (Plate xiii). It would seem hard to doubt that such a consistency of attitude indicates the nature of Kay's personal beliefs.

Kay's total output was some 900 etchings: the collection issued in 1837 includes only 340 of these, and only a handful more have been located. A few were formally exhibited during his lifetime. From 1811 to 1816 he exhibited each year with the Edinburgh Associated Artists, and in 1822 at the fourth exhibition of the Institute for the Encouragement of the Fine Arts in Scotland. In this year he made his last etching, the portrait of Archibald Campbell we reproduce here as Plate 96.

Four years later, at the age of 84, he died on 21 February 1826. He was buried in Greyfriars Churchyard alongside many of his subjects. A brief description, made towards the end of his life, tells us of 'a slender, straight old man, of middle size, and usually dressed in a garb of antique cut, of simple habits and quiet unassuming manners'.

As regards other facets of his character, we must go back to his pictures. Their gentle humour, their affectionate sympathy, their love of the curious and the eccentric, their neatness of observation and orderliness of arrangement, their simplicity of design and truthfulness of detail – all these, it is impossible to doubt, are as characteristic of the artist as they are of his art.

4

John Kay's Art

Almost nothing has ever been written about John Kay or his work. As it happens, his etchings speak so eloquently for themselves that a critic might well feel he was superfluous: but the neglect of Kay's work goes beyond this. His name is not found in most art histories, nor are his etchings reproduced even in books devoted to the black-and-white arts.

On the other hand, his prints *are* fairly frequently used to illustrate history books and studies of Scottish social conditions – often without acknowledgement. Thus in the 1870s a book was published entitled *Old Edinburgh Beaux & Belles* which was illustrated with 15 of Kay's portraits – yet the artist's name does not appear once in the book, neither on the title-page nor elsewhere.

Kay's popularity with the historians is certainly related to his neglect by the critics. To the latter, when they have given him any heed at all, he is a freak, someone outside the main stream and too awkward to fit into tidy categories: a self-taught amateur with negligible artistic skill, who can be safely passed over. To the historians, on the other hand, he is a unique chronicler and faithful delineator of his time and place. Yet simple reasoning should have shown that Kay could never have fulfilled his role *vis-a-vis* the historians so excellently, had he not possessed skills deserving the respect of the critics also.

From the historians' point of view, naturally, the faithfulness of Kay's portraiture is of supreme importance. Few as his commentators have been, they unanimously agree on one thing, that his portraits are unquestionably true to their originals. Robert Chambers, in his *Biographical Dictionary of Eminent Scotsmen*, says:

> To speak of his portraits as caricatures is doing them signal injustice. They were the most exact and faithful likenesses that could have been reproduced by any mode of art. He drew the man as he walked the street every day; his gait, his costume, every peculiarity of his appearance, done to a point, and no defect perceptible except the stiffness of the figures.

So the first and most fundamental of Kay's talents is his knack of putting a recognisable likeness of people down on paper. Where or how he acquired this knack is one of the mysteries of art, the sort of mystery for which phrases like 'heaven-sent' were coined as a substitute for explanation. But such a gift is not so common that the critics can afford to overlook it. A barber might be expected to take more than an average interest in the human face and form, but that alone does not make him a portrait artist. Even if Kay had no other skill, his ability to catch a likeness would seem to merit critical recognition.

In general, collections of portraits, however brilliant and however faithful, tend to be repetitive. One of the remarkable characteristics of Kay's work is that, though the greater number of his etchings are straightforward portraits with no background or other apparatus, they none the less offer a very striking

xvi The Earl of Eglinton

variety. Not in the way they are drawn, but in the way they are presented. The approach he took to each of his subjects was chosen, whether consciously or intuitively, to bring out the point he wanted to make. The visual information is there, solidly and assuredly, but 'edited' by the artist's perception and discrimination.

It is true, this variety of Kay's is largely one of fancy. There is no great profundity to it, it is largely a matter of arranging the figures in the frame, of varying angles and adjusting shapes. But at the level at which Kay was working, this is not to find fault. The art of the caricaturist – and this is what Kay primarily was – must inevitably be first and foremost a superficial one. No doubt the greater the caricaturist, the greater the depths he is able to express. But he must always lead us to those depths by way of the surface, and must never skip the primary message.

There is no question that as a satirist Kay was effective. A man is not cudgelled or taken to court unless he has struck at his target with a high degree of accuracy. For the most part, we today cannot feel his bite, we can only enjoy his humour. For most of us, it is the humour of Kay's work which is its first appeal: and only a few would deny that this remains their most important single ingredient. They were, after all, intended to entertain. That they continue to do so, even now that their subjects are dead and largely forgotten, is a tribute to the universality of the subject-matter Kay chose to depict, proof that while lampooning the individual he was really drawing our attention to universal traits: the mark of the true satirist.

xvii Lord Kames, Hugo Arnot and Lord Monboddo

What is peculiarly characteristic of Kay's humour is the human interest, sympathy and often patent affection which his portraits reveal. Even when he is mocking his subject, we find none of the venom and virulence of his great contemporaries Rowlandson or Gillray. Kay never loses his cool. We can hardly suppose that he personally felt fond of all his subjects, and yet there is not one who is drawn with spite or savagery. In most, on the contrary, there is a discernible sympathy for his subject, a recognition of his failings as not merely tolerable but positively endearing, which gives the man individuality and without which, Kay asks us to agree, he would be the poorer. As examples, note especially his portraits of criminals; notably that of Deacon Brodie the respectable burglar (Plate 18), where the artist simply sets aside the criminality to show us the man himself: and even that of James M'Kean, a particularly callous murderer (Plate 54).

Time and time again, Kay invites us to share his own sense of wonder at the marvellous variety of humankind. The caption to Plate 17 could stand as an epigraph for all his work: 'I say, we are fearfully and wonderfully made.' Cool and poised, elegant and detached, Kay's prints are the perfect reflection of the climate of Edinburgh society of his day. If we regard this as a defect in him, that he lacked the political commitment, the force and vigour that animated Gillray and the others, then we must level the same criticism at the society in which he lived and worked. For many, the quiet incisive statement of the Scotsman's message is ultimately more persuasive than the heavy-handed hammer-blows of the London caricaturists of the day.

At the same time, these characteristics of his work must surely also reflect the artist's own temperament. It is impossible to believe that Kay's style is anything but a direct expression of his own personality. The neatness of

xviii Sir James Montgomery and David Stuart Moncrief

execution, the economy of line, the absence of unnecessary detail – all, surely, reflect a similar cast of mind in the artist himself. If we could visit his shop, we would find it orderly as a museum; if we could visit his workroom, we would find the tools on his etching bench meticulously arranged in their proper order.

His style is all the more surely an expression of his own nature, in that he had no artistic training. Sir Herbert Maxwell (in his history of Edinburgh) lays himself open to the easiest of rejoinders when he writes, as illogically as ungrammatically: 'Being entirely self-taught, Kay's work is of negligible artistic merit.' Perhaps this fact in his life is another contributory factor to the neglect his work encountered, and helps to explain if not to excuse such strictures as this by J M Gray in the *Magazine of Art* in the 1880s:

> With few exceptions they must be pronounced failures, if we regard them simply as examples of the art of etching.

or this from the *Encyclopedia Britannica* (Ninth Edition):

> The caricatures have little strictly artistic merit, beyond their graphic power.

It is apparent that even these critics hesitated to condemn outright: they felt the force of Kay's work, even though their rule-books told them that Kay could not be eligible for the artistic laurels. We, who are lucky enough to live in an age when the rule-books have lost their old authority, can only thank providence for depriving him of a formal artistic education. A teacher could have taught him nothing that would have added to the effect of his work, would almost certainly have inhibited that intuitive simplicity.

For the strength of Kay's work is essentially that of the naïve or primitive artist. His conception of the artist's function is childishly simple: he goes directly to his subject; he tells us what he wants us to know about that subject; then he stops. Every line, every detail, is there to do a job. Nothing is superfluous.

xix Man with a stick: an ink drawing by Kay, the first stage of one of his portraits

The same considerations apply to the way he composed his pictures. If he thinks he can tell us more by showing his subject in full, he gives us a full-length. Alternatively, he may cut his figures off at any suitable point – as in the three plates reproduced here (Plates xvi, xvii and xviii). The cutting-off of the figures is a brilliant *tour de force* which concentrates our interest precisely where Kay wants it. By any textbook criterion the compositions are unconventional and improper; by the criterion of whether or not they help the artist to achieve his purpose, they reveal a simple and invincible logic.

The result of this direct approach was that Kay often anticipates the more conscious innovations of later artists. Picking two plates almost at random, those of Miss Luckie

xx The Beggers' feast: after Ostade. A copy made by Kay just as he was setting out on his career as artist

Smith (Plate 50) and Fergusson & Boruwlaski (Plate 71), we find a sense of composition and placing for which it is hard to find an equal until the great black-and-white revolution of the 1890s. And Kay can even claim one merit over those later artists, in that he never sacrifices his subject for the sake of the composition. To return to our starting-point, his portraits remain true likenesses, no matter what contrivances he employs: if they are presented within a compositional *tour de force*, it is because their subjects demand precisely that of him.

The consistency of Kay's style throughout his career – it is virtually impossible to date a print except where he has had the forethought to date it for us – is a further indication of how naturally his style came to him. Once he had discovered and perfected his technique, he never saw any reason to modify it or trade it in for anything different, throughout 40 years of active artistic life. The only discernible development is from broad effects to more subtle, from harder drawing to softer, from angular shapes to gentler – in short, from caricature to naturalism. Such etchings as Plates 91 and 94, done in 1815–1816, reveal a maturity of which he would not have been capable back in the 1780s; yet his portrait of Latour (Plate 89, done in 1813) is almost a companion-piece to his own self-portrait of 1786 (Plate viii).

Kay's work has its limitations, of course. Chambers rightly puts his finger on one of them when he refers to 'the stiffness of the figures'. If Kay never loses his own cool, nor does he allow his subjects to dispense with theirs; and we may further suspect that if in life they lacked it, he lent them some of his own. Each of Kay's subjects is required to become part of his world – a neat, elegant, charming, formal world where passions are kept within civilised bounds and enthusiasm is received with a gently tolerant smile. Should we complain? We have not the right; it is his privilege. Kay drew what he wanted to draw, and in the way he saw it. And in the end, like every true artist, he created a world in his own image.

5

Plates

All the plates in
duced the same s
exception of 75 a
slightly reduced i

Numbers iii, i
in the text have
page layout.

Notes to the p
35 to 50.

plate 1

plate 2

DOUGLAS
La. RAN. Eternal providence! What is thy name?
My name is NORVAL: and my name he bears.
J. Kay fec.t 1784

plate 3

plate 4

Let Puppy's bark, and Aſses bray,
Each Dog, and Cur will have his day,

plate 5

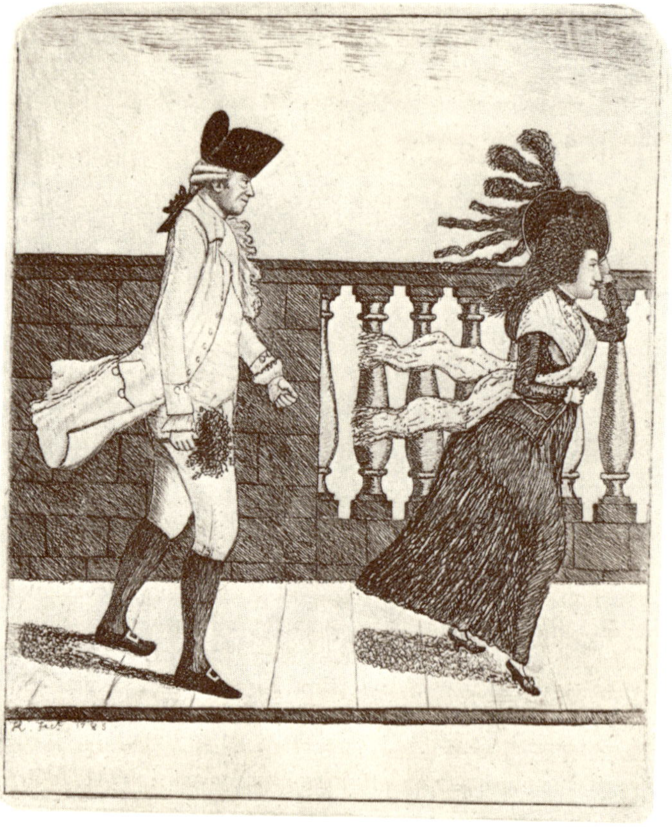

plate 6

plate 7

K fec.
1785
Thus we poor Cooks, exert our Skill & Brav'ry
For idle Gulls, and Kites, that trade in Knav'ry

plate 8

Why, Sir John, my face does you no harm. No, I'll be ſworn; I make as good uſe of it many
man does of a death's head, or a memento mori. I never ſee thy noſe, but I think upon

plate 9

plate 10

Duke and Duchess
of Braganza

plate 12

plate 13

plate 14

plate 15

plate 16

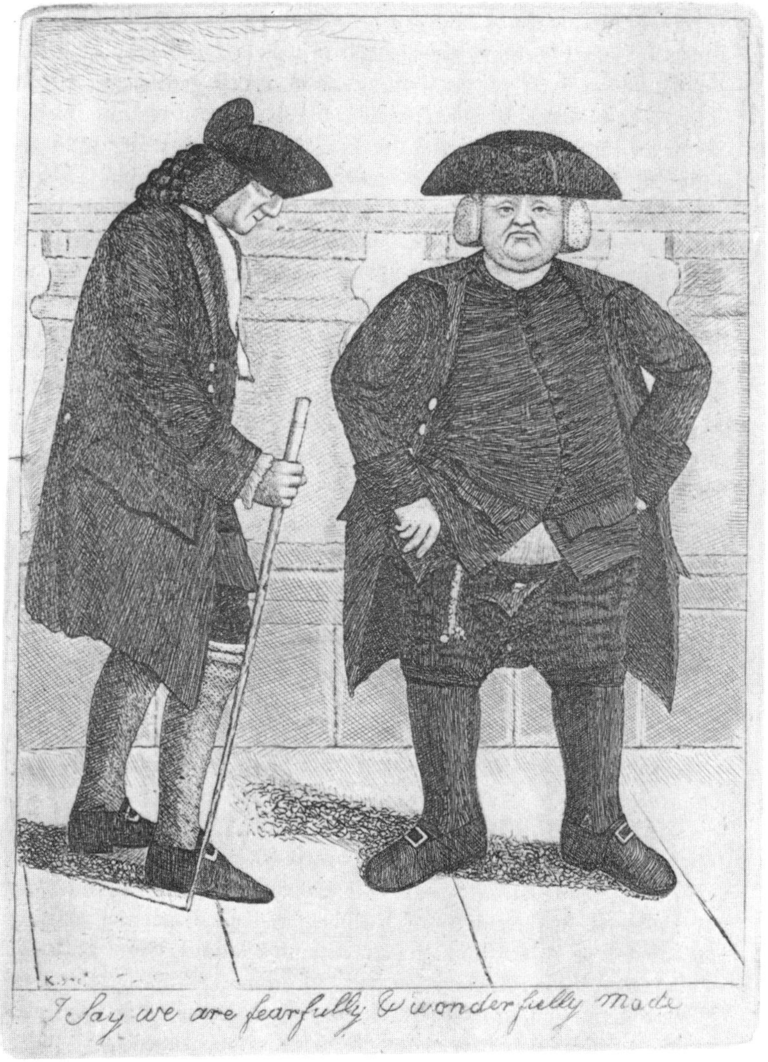
I Say we are fearfully & wonderfully made

plate 17

The First Interview in 1786

plate 18

plate 19

I PRAY FOR ALL
I PLEAD FOR ALL
I MAINTAIN ALL
I FIGHT FOR ALL
I TAKE ALL
THE FIVE ALL'S
I. KAY. DEL. SCULP.

plate 20

Burns whose Beauty warms the age
and fills our Youth with love & rage

plate 21

plate 22

SAM. *A Soldier I am for a Lady, what Beau was ere arm'd compleater &c*

plate 23

AFTER MARRIAGE
K. 1789
BEFORE MARRIAGE
K. 1789

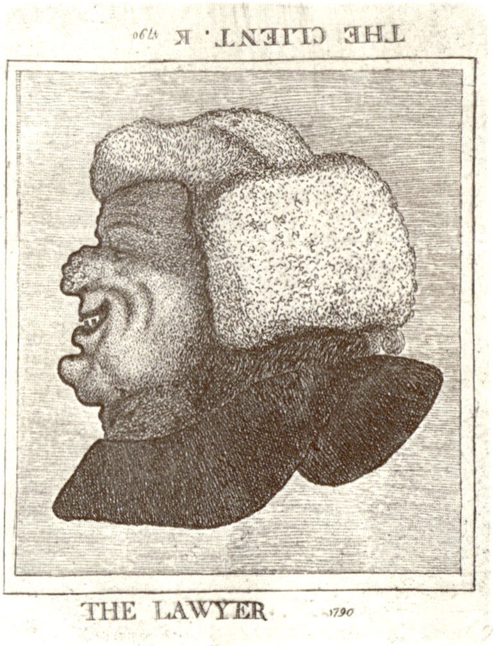
THE CLIENT. K 1790
THE LAWYER
1790

plate 24

plate 25

KNIGHT of the TURF

plate 26

This represents old Geordy Sime
a Famous Piper in his time

plate 27

The Author of the Wealth of Nations

plate 28

plate 29

KAY
NINTY FOUR YEARS HAVE I
SOJOURNED UPON THIS EARTH
ENDEAVOURING TO DO GOOD

plate 30

Travells Eldest Son in Conversation with a Cherokee Chief.
How dare you approach me with your travells. There is not a single word of them true
There you may be right, and altho I never dined upon the Lion or eat half a Cow and turned the rest to grafs, yet my works have been of more use to mankind than yours and there is more truth in one page of my Edin.r directory than in all your five Volumes 4°. So when you talk to me dont imagine yourfelf at the Source of the Nile!
J. Kay Del. et Sculp.t Publifhed as the Act Directs 179

plate 31

A. HIGHLAND CHIEFTAIN

plate 32

The Scottish Patriot.

plate 33

plate 34

plate 35

PATENT for KNIGHTHOOD.

plate 36

plate 37

Thats Your Sort!!!
The Brisk Widow;; and the tight Lad. or
M.r & M.rs Lee Lewes in the Road to Ruin.

plate 38

plate 39

plate 40

plate 41

EDIN.R ROYAL VOLUNTEERS.

plate 42

plate 43

plate 44

LEITH VOLUNTEER.

plate 45

I.Kay fecit 1795
PETTICOAT GOVERNMENT
or
the Gray mare is the Better Horse.

plate 46

plate 47

Mr. H. E. JOHNSTON
IN THE CHARACTER OF HAMLET.
"That undiscover'd Country, from whose bourne no traveller returns.
I Kay fecit 1795

plate 48

plate 49

Original, Price One Pound One

plate 50

GENEROUS SPORTSMAN.

plate 52

plate 53

plate 54

plate 55

TURN-COATS AND CUT-THROATS.

plate 56

plate 57

plate 58

TO THE RIGHT ABOUT—FACE

plate 59

I.K. 1797

Dedicated to the Royal Edin^r. Light Dragoons.

plate 60

Copper-bottom's retreat, or a View of Carron Work!!!

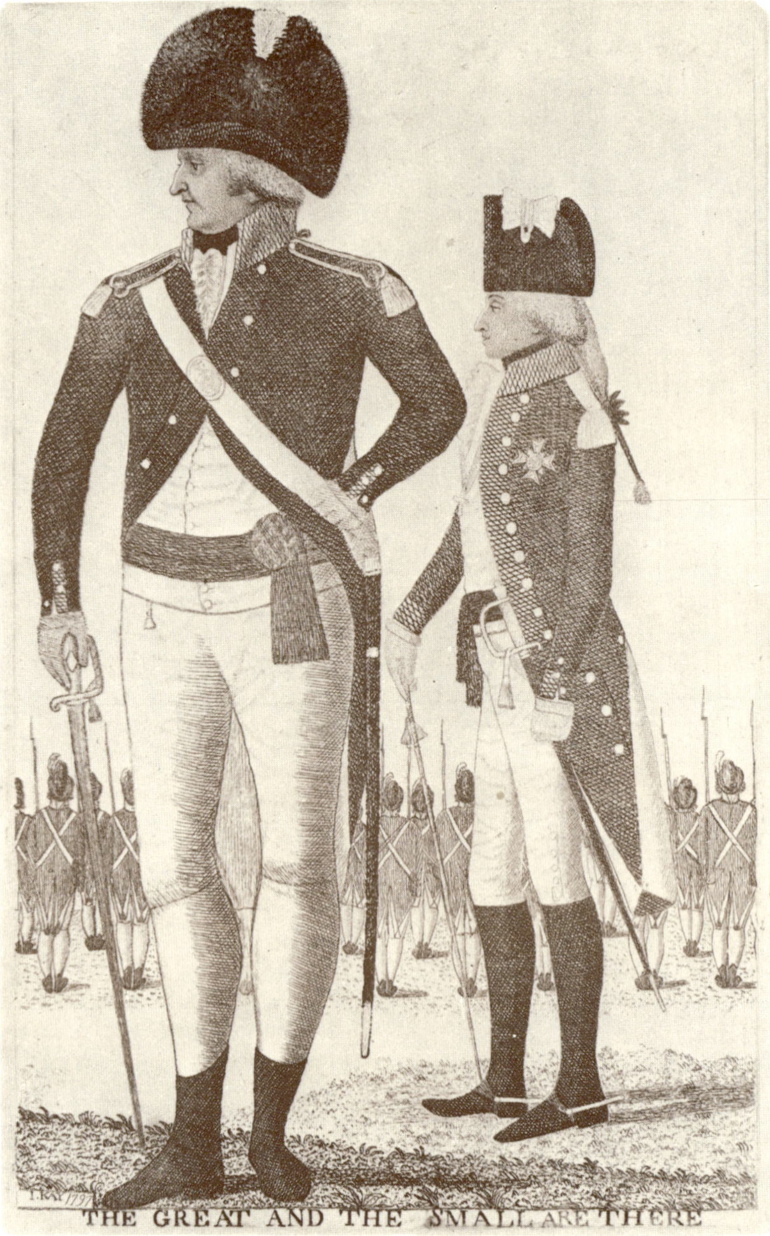
I Kay 1797
THE GREAT AND THE SMALL ARE THERE

plate 62

plate 63

plate 64

plate 65

plate 66

THE FORTUNATE DUELIST

plate 67

Wha'l buy my lucky forpit o' Sa-a't. Na: Na: it 'ill nae doe: Deel ane yet.

plate 68

Drawn & etched by I Kay No. 10 Parliat. Close Edinr. 1800.

plate 70

plate 71

plate 72

TOUSSAINT LOUVERTURE

plate 73

plate 74

Mr. OBRIEN the IRISH GIANT the TALLEST MAN IN the KNOWN WORLD BEING NEAR NINE FEET HIGH

plate 75

By the la' Harry
This shall not go for Nothing

COCK OF THE GREEN.

plate 76

WILL^M. MACDONALD
Officer to the
HIGHLAND SOCIETY of SCOTLAND

THE LATE EMPEROR PAUL

plate 78

INVERNESS-SHIRE MILITIA

plate 79

AN EMINENT JUDGE
OF BROOM BESOMS !!!
Old JOHN TAIT the Besom maker who Travelled the Country
begging and Selling Besoms till he arrived at the age of one hundred & ten years Died in Jan.y 1772
Leaving YOUNG JOHN, and 27 other Descendants

From an Original Print by J. K.

plate 80

plate 81

John Steel of the Parish of Little Dunkeld Perthshire Aged 109 drawn from the Life

plate 82

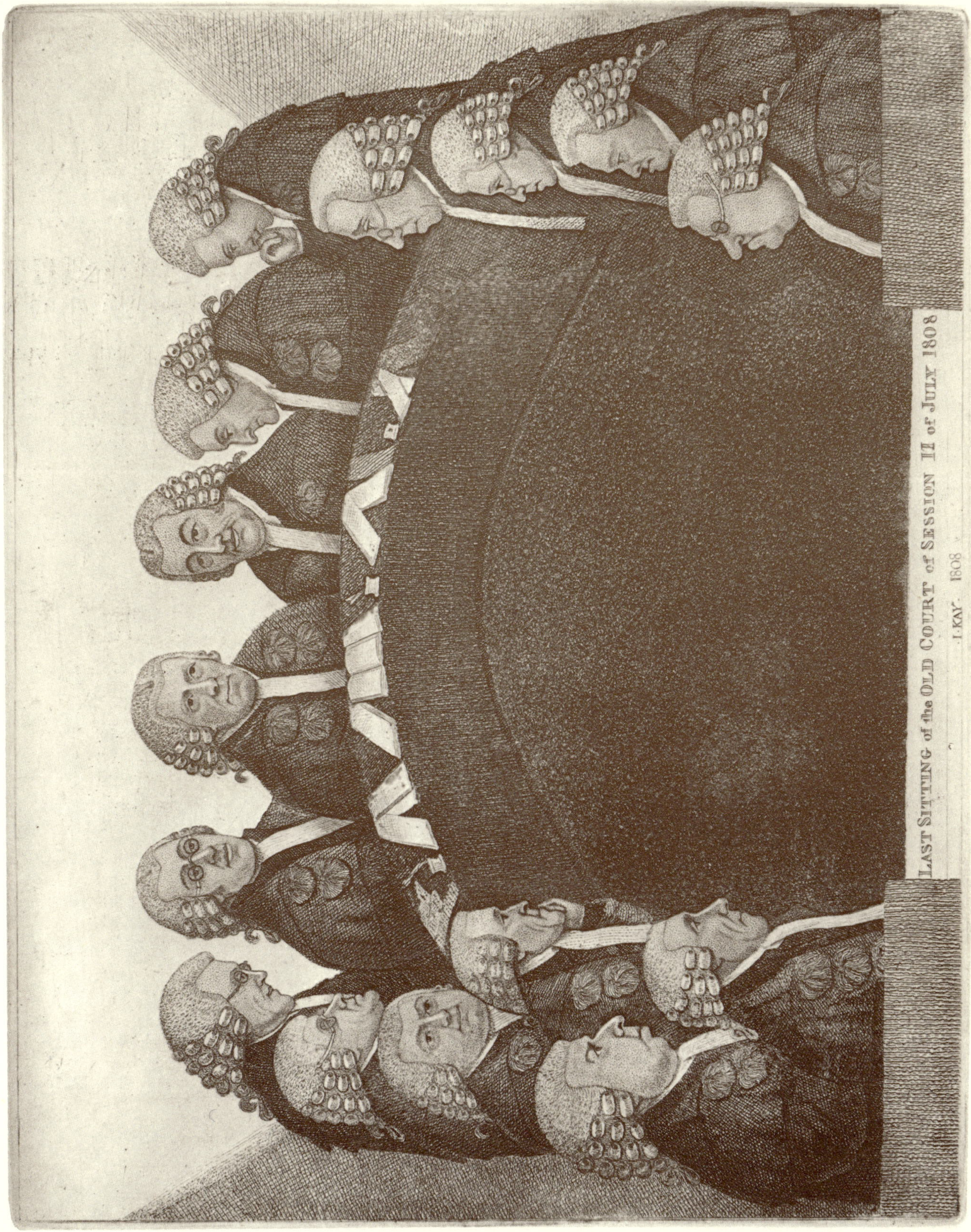
LAST SITTING of the OLD COURT of SESSION 11 of JULY 1808
I. KAY. 1808

plate 83

M^c. ARTHUR, *PIPER*
To RANALD MACDONALD Esq^R. of STAFFA

plate 84

JOHN KNOX
THE SCOTISH REFORMER
BORN A.D. 1505 . DIED . 1572.
From an Original Picture

plate 85

plate 86

I KAY 1811
ADVOCATES

WHA'L O CALLER OYSTERS

plate 88

plate 89

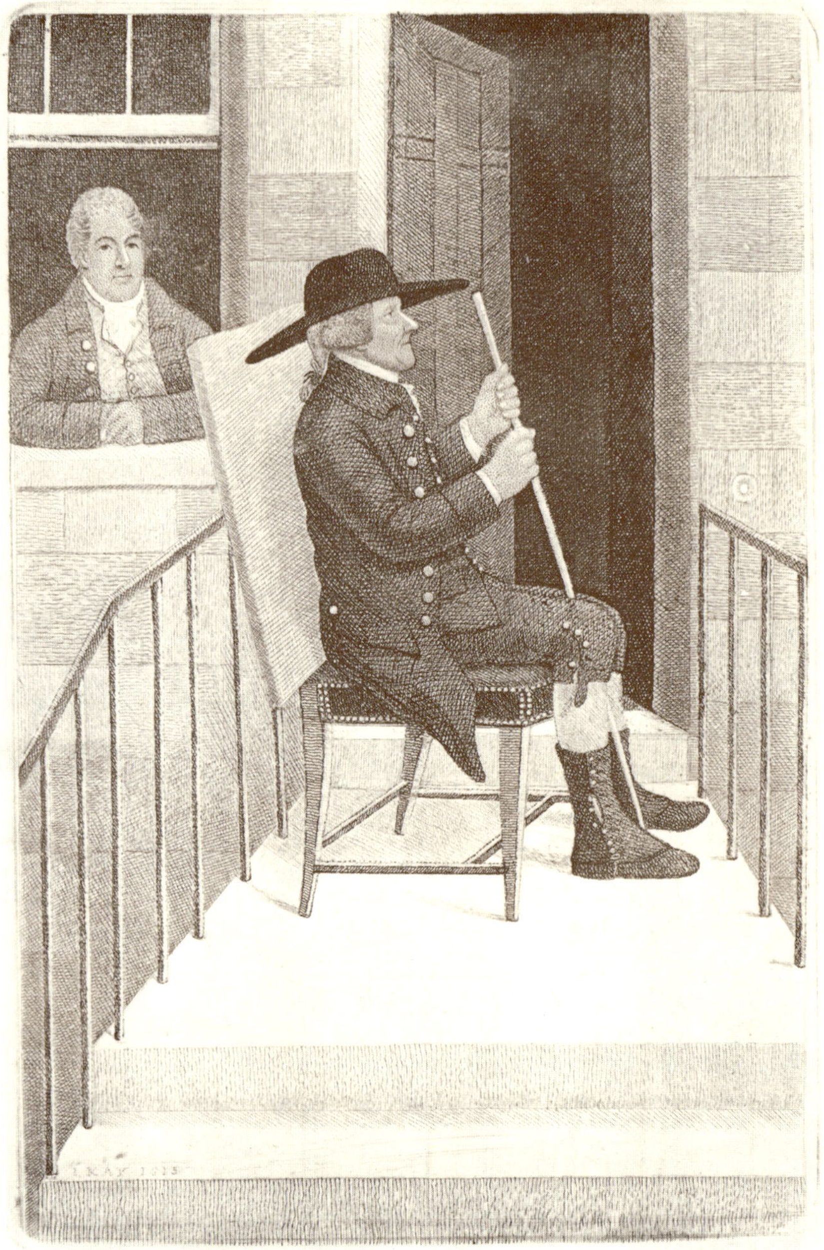

plate 90

WILL.^M WILSON. *Commonly called*
Mortar Willie. Aged. 107.

I KAY 1815.

plate 91

plate 92

plate 93

ISOBEL TAYLOR Aged 105 widow of JOHN ALICE
She was Born in the parish of Crieff County of Perth the 4th of March 1713.
and died in Edinr the 23rd of April 1818.

plate 94

plate 95

plate 96

6

Notes on the Illustrations

The illustrations to the textual chapters, frontispiece and endpapers, are numbered i–xx; those in the Plates section are numbered 1–96. Unless otherwise indicated, the illustrations are from Paton's edition of Kay's *Original Portraits* (1837). A number such as '2/53' indicates that the plate is number 53 in Paton's second volume: 'sup' indicates that the plate is from the group of supplementary plates added to some editions.

The dates are those provided by Kay himself, and refer to the etching rather than the original drawing. In most cases we may assume that etching followed closely after drawing, but in some cases it may well be that a considerable time may have elapsed.

The notes provided here have been kept as brief as possible, and include only such information as is likely to be positively helpful to the appreciation of the picture. There are full descriptive notes regarding the subject-matter of Kay's prints in Paton's book, though little will be found there regarding Kay's work, or his attitude to or involvement with the subject.

i *Frontispiece* **Self-portrait with print**
Oil, 247 × 190 mm. Courtesy Scottish National Portrait Gallery, Catalogue number 892.

Kay's two other self-portraits (see Plates iii and viii) are dated 1786 and 1788 respectively. Judging by appearances, this oil painting dates from the same period, when the artist in his mid-forties was enjoying the first fruits of success in his new way of life.

ii *End-papers* **The Parliament Close and Public Characters of Edinburgh 50 years since**

Published 1 October 1844. Engraved by Le Conte, etched by Thomas Dobbie, published by Alexander Hill of 67 Princes Street. Courtesy Scottish National Portrait Gallery, Catalogue number SPL 174/1 (key SPL IV 737–1).

This very interesting mixed etching and aquatint is taken from a striking oil painting in the collection at the Huntly House Museum, Edinburgh: the painting was itself the joint production of Sir David Wilkie, Alexander Nasmyth, David Roberts, Clarkson Stanfield, James Wilson and two others named Frazer and Williamson. Precisely what part each member of this septemvirate played in the proceedings defies the imagination, and perhaps the sheer length of the credit list explains why nobody found space to mention Kay, though in fact his originals are used for the majority of the figures to be seen in the Close, and who are identified in the accompanying Key. The Edinburgh Public Library possesses another copy of the engraving, together with an interesting early proof of the etched portion, before the application of the aquatint, which has the effect of throwing Kay's figures into greater prominence. Whether or not Wilkie and his collaborators realised it, the view represented in the engraving must approximate fairly closely to that which Kay would see through the window of his shop.

iii **Self-portrait at easel**
Water-colour, approx. 120 × 180 mm. Courtesy Royal Scottish Academy.

This most informative portrait is from the folio of his works described in the Bibliography. A wood engraving was made for The Magazine of Art around 1890, but so far as is known the picture itself has never been reproduced before. Amongst other things, it tells us that Kay's work in oils was not confined to the self-portrait we reproduce as our frontispiece: knowing his punctiliousness in signing his work, it should not be difficult for the present owners of any of Kay's work to identify it.

iv **Edinburgh in 1779**
Copper engraving, 81 × 314 mm, from Cooke's Modern Universal Traveller. Courtesy Mary Evans Picture Library.

This view conveys perfectly the compact character of the city when Kay first came to work there.

v **Edinburgh High Street in the early nineteenth century**
Lithograph by T Picken from a drawing by Leitch. Courtesy Mary Evans Picture Library.

A good view of the centre of Edinburgh, when Kay lived and worked there. His house was one of those in the far distance on the left-hand side of the street: his shop was on the right, behind St Giles' cathedral which can be seen jutting out into the street.

vi **Part of the Old Town, Edinburgh**
Steel engraving by Lacey after drawing by Thomas Shepherd, 1829. Courtesy Mary Evans Picture Library.

Although drawn a year or two after Kay's death, this represents substantially the Edinburgh that the artist knew. It shows vividly how the buildings of the Old Town clustered round the High Street which runs up the ridge of the hill towards the Castle (which is just to the right of the picture). Kay's house would be just behind the very tall tenements on the left of the print, and his shop was of course behind the tower of St Giles' which dominates the skyline. The eastern causeway in the foreground is the Mound where the Scottish National Gallery and Academy now stand, each housing a few examples of his work.

vii **Fireman and linkboy**
Watercolour by John Kay. Courtesy Scottish National Gallery.

viii **Self-portrait with cat**
1786 Paton 1/1

Kay has himself supplied a descriptive note for this print: 'Our author has drawn himself, in this Print, sitting in a thoughtful posture, in an antiquated chair (whereby he means to represent his love of antiquities) with his favourite cat (the largest it is believed in Scotland) sitting upon the back of it; several pictures hanging behind him; a bust of Homer, with his painting utensils on the table before him, a scroll of paper in his hand, and a volume of his works upon his knee.' Precisely what he intends by the phrase 'a volume of his works' excites conjecture: so far as is known nothing was published during his lifetime, so perhaps this merely represents the volume he *hoped* to bring out, and for which this note was intended.

ix **Self-portrait miniature**
1788 Sup/27

x and xi **Hamilton Bell's wager,** and **The Artist under Examination**
1792 2/94 and 2/96

Hamilton Bell was a Writer to the Signet but, like many other professional men in Edinburgh at that time, he 'conducted his business chiefly in taverns'. One day he made a wager to walk the 7 miles from Edinburgh to Musselburgh carrying the pot-boy on his back. The feat was accomplished in the early hours of the morning, passing the fish-women on their way to Edinburgh market. For some reason, Bell took offence at the publication of Kay's print, and obtained an interdict prohibiting its sale. However Kay successfully satisfied the Sheriff that his print showed nothing but the truth, and the interdict was dropped, much to the chagrin of Bell (second from left) and his second.

xii **A scene in the Caricature Ware Room, Edinburgh, 1796**
Courtesy Mary Evans Picture Library.

We can only speculate about the origin of this extremely interesting print, which clearly shows the artist defending himself against an outraged victim. The scene is evidently Kay's own shop in Parliament Close, for a corner of St Giles' Cathedral can be seen through the left-hand window. The identity of the victim is uncertain: the closest resemblance to anyone in 'Edinburgh Portraits' is to George, 14th Earl of Errol, who as it happens was in the news in 1796. But we know of no etching which corresponds with the one held by Kay's visitor, nor of any reason why the noble lord should have taken offence at Kay's etching.

xiii **The Modern Cain's Lament**
1798 2/86

A satire against William Pitt when hostilities were being undertaken against the French Republic – a rare political subject which gives us a clue to Kay's personal views. The 'Harrie' to whom Pitt is complaining is his friend Henry Dundas, later Lord Melville, a prominent Edinburgh citizen.

xiv **The City Guard**
Etching, 300 × 435 mm. Courtesy Edinburgh Public Libraries.

This curious etching can hardly be by John Kay himself, but no less clearly is it a conscious attempt to imitate his style – indeed, we include it here to demonstrate just how inimitable that style was! It could be the product of his eldest son William, except that it is technically so inferior – and surely technique, if nothing else, William would have acquired from his father? In any case, it is inferior even to the two plates by William which are included in the collection of his father's etchings (see note to the following plate).

xv **The Evening Walk**
Etching by William Kay. Courtesy Royal Scottish Academy.

This etching, though broadly reminiscent of John Kay, is signed by his son and betrays its origin in any case by its deficient skill. Two of the plates in Paton's collection of John Kay's work – The City Tronmen (2/54) and The Social Pinch (Two Chairmen) (2/122) – are also in fact etched by William, which accounts for their marked inferiority to the rest of the collection. Interestingly enough, an earlier state of The Social Pinch, in the authors' collection, is signed W Kay, but when reproduced in Paton's collection an 'I' was added before the W ('I' and 'J' were of course interchangeable at this date). Whether the intention was to delude readers into believing the print to be John's work we cannot say, but if so it was successful – though quite unaccountably so, considering the blatant inferiority of the work.

xvi **The Earl of Eglinton**
1793 2/44

xvii **Lord Kames, Hugo Arnot and Lord Monboddo**
1784 1/5

xviii **Sir James Montgomery and David Stuart Moncrief**
1788 1/79

These three plates have been chosen to illustrate Kay's original use of 'cropping techniques' – concentrating the interest by eliminating the irrelevant, even to the point of truncating the anatomy! The effect is excitingly 'modern', and most successful.

xix **Man with a stick**
Ink drawing. Courtesy Royal Scottish Academy.

A first sketch by John Kay, presumably the initial stage in the process of making a portrait.

xx **The Beggars' Feast**
1784 Sup/24

This etching after Ostade was made when Kay was just on the threshold of his new career. It seems reasonable to guess that it was intended as an exercise, proving to himself – and perhaps to his patron – that he had the necessary skill. Setting aside the fact that Kay had had no artistic training whatever, the piece amply refutes those who have suggested that his work is deficient in technical skill. Only by very high professional standards could this work of a self-taught amateur be faulted.

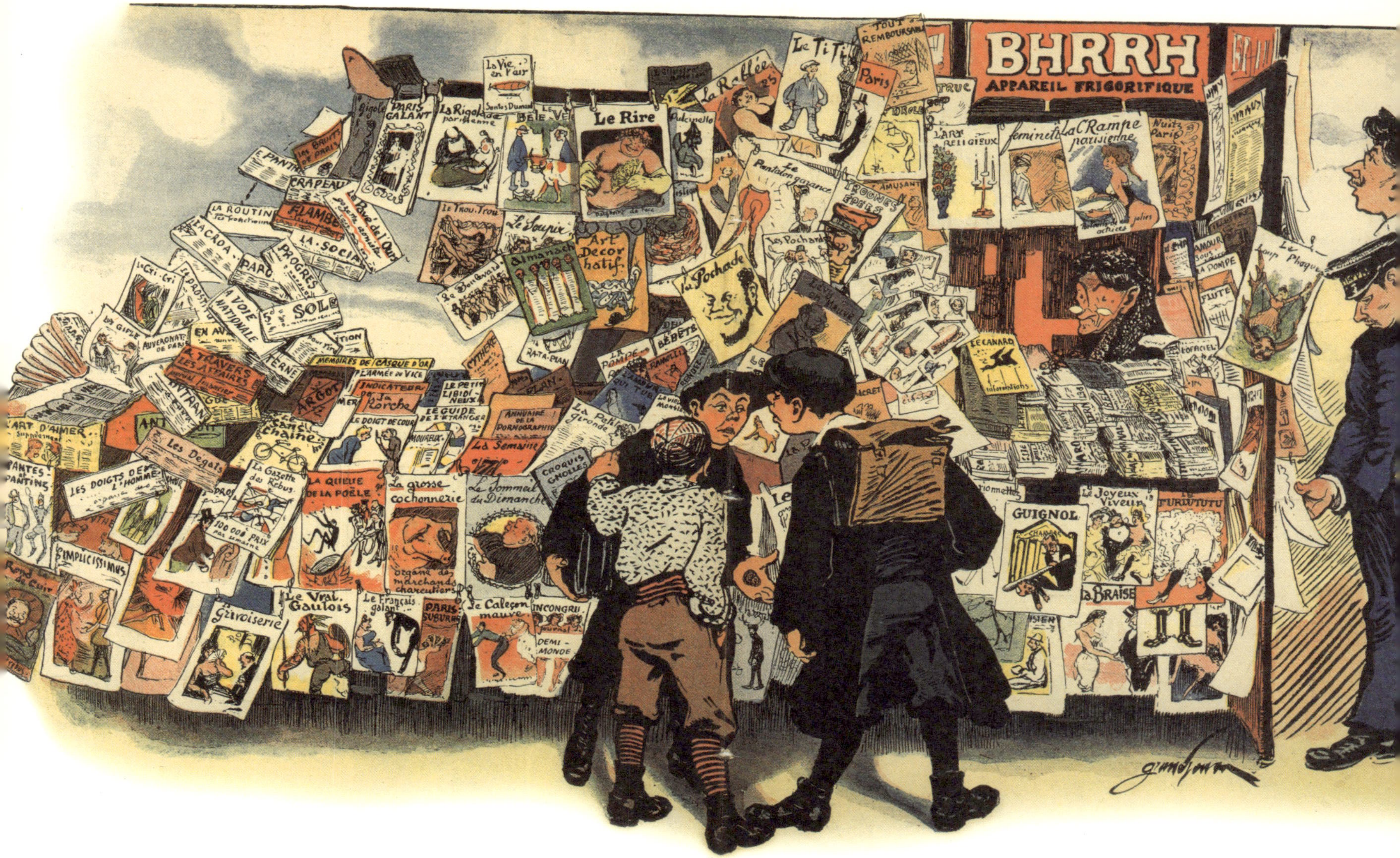

French boys buying 'girlie' magazines, *Le Rire*, 1902.

Self-portrait by John Kay, 1796, who depicted Edinburgh life and society at the end of the 18th century.

1 **Three Giants, with a group of spectators**
1784 1/4

These three men were all Irish, and all visited Edinburgh – though not together, as Kay shows them. Charles Byrne, at 2.49 m (8 ft 2 in), was the tallest: the two others were twins, nearly 8 feet tall. During his visit to Edinburgh, Byrne is said to have alarmed the watchmen on the North Bridge by lighting his pipe at a street-lamp.

2 **Dr Glen and the Daft Highland Laird**
1784 1/9

Kay has placed together two noted eccentrics of Edinburgh. On the left is Dr Glen, a citizen who had his reputed national trait in an extreme form – though exceedingly wealthy, he inquired if a second-hand coffin could be procured when burying his wife. His companion is James Robertson of Kincraigie, a fervent Jacobite who had been imprisoned for a short while for the part he took in the '45 rebellion. For some reason this affected his reason, and it became his ambition to be hanged, drawn and quartered as a martyr to the Stuart cause. To this end he shouted treason against the House of Hanover in the street, drank toasts openly to Bonny Prince Charlie – but all in vain, since everyone knew of his affliction. Eventually he managed to get himself in gaol, for not paying his rent: even though friends speedily paid it for him, he refused to leave: ultimately he was tricked into freedom by being informed his case was to be tried, whereupon he agreed to leave the prison en route – as he supposed – for the courts. Once in the street, he found the prison door slammed in his face – and the gaoler deaf to all entreaties to re-admit him! After that he took to carving in wood the heads of public personages he liked or disliked, which he held up to public view as he walked about. He carved a fresh one each day: following the appearance of this print, he retaliated in his own way – when passers-by inquired about his next production, 'Don't you see it's the barber?' he replied.

3 **Mrs Siddons, Mr Sutherland and Mrs Woods in the tragedy of 'Douglas'**
1784 1/55

Mrs Siddons visited Edinburgh in May 1784 and was a fantastic success – 'the rage for seeing her was so great, that one day there were 25,587 applications for 630 places'. The scene portrayed by Kay had such an effect that the *Edinburgh Courant* found itself unable to avoid the obvious: 'we believe there was not a dry eye in the whole house'.

4 **Courtship**
1784 1/60

This print was done as a joke at the time that Kay was courting his second wife. It was probably influenced by the Flemish caricaturists, with whose work we know from his Ostade imitation that he must have been familiar. But there is a sense of sympathy behind the drawing which effectively mitigates the ugliness of the features.

5 **A medley of musicians**
1784 2/34

This satire was produced as retaliation for a caricature of Kay drawn by one of the subjects.

6 **Dr James Graham going along the North Bridge in a High Wind**
1785 1/11

Dr Graham was a noted practitioner of early fringe medicine: he founded a Temple of Health & Hymen in Pall Mall, furnished with a 'grand celestial bed' and 'magnificent electrical apparatus' which he later moved to Edinburgh. Of his lectures, a contemporary wrote to the *Westminster Magazine*: 'The nature of the subject naturally obliges him to border on what is generally termed indelicacy; but he always endeavours to guard his audience against imbibing sentiments in any respect repugnant to virtue, chastity, and modest deportment; he earnestly recommends marriage as honourable in all, and as strongly execrates prostitution and criminality; wherein then is he to blame?' In view of such an enconium, one can only conjecture why Kay chose to portray him in apparent pursuit of a lady.

7 **Vincent Lunardi in his balloon**
1785 1/36

The celebrated Italian balloonist visited Edinburgh in 1785, and made his first ascent on 5 October from the green of Heriot's Hospital. Shops were shut, business virtually ceased, and some 80,000 spectators gathered to watch. Lunardi rose like a sky-rocket, and flew some 80 km in $1\frac{1}{2}$ hours – a flight not surpassed in Scotland for more than half a century. On a second flight, two months later, he landed close to the home of Kay's patron at Dirleton, and was taken there as an honoured guest. In compliment to Lunardi, the Scottish ladies took to wearing 'Lunardi bonnets' of thin gauze, stretched on wire to resemble a balloon.

8 **Cockfight**
1785 1/44

This plate depicts an actual match, between Lanark and Haddington counties, at which many prominent Edinburgh citizens were present. Kay's own comment is: 'It cannot but appear surprising that noblemen and gentlemen, who upon any other occasion will hardly show the smallest degree of condescension to their inferiors, will, in the prosecution of this barbarous amusement, demean themselves so far as to associate with the very lowest characters in society.' Once again, an interesting insight to Kay's own views and feelings.

9 **Mr Henderson and Mr Charteris as Falstaff and Bardolph in Shakespeare's Henry IV**
1785 1/63

10 **Levelling of the High Street of Edinburgh**
1785 1/93

This valuable operation, part of the great programme of municipal improvements carried out in the latter half of the eighteenth century, was nevertheless the subject of a hard-fought squabble between local politicians. Kay, who lived and worked there, must have had his views: but they do not appear in this print.

11 **Mr Church and Mrs Yates in Crisp's tragedy Braganza**
1785 2/71

Mrs Yates, an actress hardly less celebrated than Sarah Siddons, visited Edinburgh in 1785 and was paid 100 guineas a night for her performances! Whether the surrounding members of the audience are intended as likenesses is not known.

12 **Dr John Hope, Professor of Botany**
1785 2/141

Dr Hope was the first naturalist in Scotland to introduce the Linnaean system. He is shown directing a workman in the Botanic Garden which he caused to be laid out in Leith Walk.

13 **Robert Johnston and Sibilla Hutton, two shopkeepers**
1786 1/158

He was a banker: she was a milliner, noted for their remarkable dress. When she appeared at divine service wearing the hat shown in Kay's print, the minister was moved to remonstrate: 'Sibby! Sibby! do you really expect to get to heaven with such a bonnet on your head?' 'And why not, father?' she replied, 'I'm sure I'll make a better appearance there than you will do with that vile, old-fashioned black wig, which you have worn for these last twenty years!'

14 **Dr Joseph Black, chemist**
1787 1/23

Dr Black, of Edinburgh University, is known as the discoverer of latent heat and for other valuable work. He also had the distinction of teaching James Watt and giving him the impulse towards his epoch-making development of the steam engine.

15 **Captain Dalrymple and Penelope Macdonald of Clanronald**
1787 2/133 and 2/134

Sad to report, when they married, it was not to each other.

16 **Angelo Tremamondo, riding master**
1788 1/32

This celebrated equestrian had taught the royal Princes in London before setting up business in Edinburgh in 1768.

17 **Alexander Hunter of Polmood and Roger Hog of Newliston, two merchants**
Date unknown, probably late 1780s. 1/17

The caption is intended to be spoken by Hog, who was given to using the phrase 'I say' at the start of his speeches – and might indeed find his own corpulency fearful and wonderful.

18 **The first interview between Deacon Brodie and George Smith**
1788 1/106

William Brodie was a respectable Deacon of the Incorporation of Wrights and Masons – but he had an unfortunate penchant for gambling. To supplement his income he took up burglary, and was for some time most successful, carrying out a number of ingenious robberies with his accomplice, George Smith. Eventually, however, an informer gave the tip-off to the authorities: Brodie fled the country but was arrested in Amsterdam and extradited. His conduct during his trial and at his execution was admirably cool and self-possessed:

> 'Having put on white nightcaps, Brodie pointed to Smith to ascend the steps that led to the drop; and, in an easy manner, clapping him on the shoulder, said "George Smith, you are first in hand." Upon this Smith, whose behaviour was highly penitent and resigned, slowly ascended the steps, and was immediately followed by Brodie, who mounted with briskness and agility, and examined the dreadful apparatus with attention, and particularly the halter designed for himself. The ropes being too short tied, Brodie stepped down to the platform, and entered into conversation with his friends. . . . The rope being at last properly adjusted, he deliberately untied his neck-cloth, buttoned up his waistcoat and coat, and helped the executioner to fix the rope. He then took a friend (who stood close by him) by the hand, bade him farewell, and requested that he would acquaint the world that he was still the same, and that he died like a man. He then pulled the nightcap over his face, and placed himself in an attitude expressive of firmness and resolution. . . .'

The reason for the introduction of the dog and cock is anyone's guess: from an artistic viewpoint, they are a masterstroke.

19 **Two shadows in conversation: Lord Kames and Hugo Arnot**
1788 1/132

20 **The Five Alls**
1788 2/17

Kay applies this familiar theme, often used for inn signs, to individual Edinburgh citizens:

> 'I pray for all' – the Rev. Andrew Hunter of Tron Church, known for his wide benevolence: 'I plead for all' – Henry Erskine, known as a poor man's laywer: 'I maintain all' – James Rocheid, an enthusiastic agriculturist: 'I fight for all' – Quartermaster Taylor, a veteran of the Siege of Gibraltar.

21 **Miss Burns**
1788 2/136

Though reputed to be 'no better than she should be', this celebrated beauty successfully resisted attempts by neighbours and magistrates to banish her from the city.

22 **Francis Grose, antiquary**
1789 1/18

This famous antiquary visited Edinburgh in 1789, collecting material for his *Antiquities of Scotland.* The visit inspired Burns to write his famous lines:

> Hear, Land o' Cakes and brither Scots,
> Frae Maidenkirk to Johnny Groats,
> If there's a hole in a' your coats,
> I rede you tent it;
> A chiel's amang you takin notes,
> And, faith, he'll prent it.

23 **Samuel M'Donald and George Cranstoun**
1789 1/20

'Big Sam' was a popular Edinburgh soldier, who was allowed 2/6 a day over his rightful pay on account of his height of 2.08 m (6 ft 10 in). He didn't much care for Kay putting him in the same print with Geordie Cranstoun, a beggar whose fine singing M'Donald much admired.

24 **Marriage**
1789 1/37

Lawyer and Client
1790 Sup/18

25 **Colonel Lennox, later duke of Richmond**
1789 1/39

A popular officer, noted for having once fought a duel with the duke of York.

26 **Sir Archibald Hope of Pinkie**
1789 1/126

A well-known country gentleman, and President of the exclusive Caledonian Hunt.

27 **Geordie Syme, the piper**
1789 2/48

As official Piper of Dalkeith, Syme was a retainer of the noble house of Buccleugh: as such, he 'had to attend the family on all particular occasions, and make the round of the town twice daily, at eight o'clock evening, and five in the morning.'

28 **Adam Smith, author of 'The Wealth of Nations'**
1790 1/34

Apart from a rather uninteresting medallion, Kay's etching is the only authentic likeness of the famous economist. He also appears in another Kay print (1/33).

29 **Captain Hind**
1790 1/70

Officer of the 55th regiment of foot. He was an admirer of a celebrated beauty also illustrated in this selection: but for some reason Kay's annotator does not tell us which. Our guess is Miss Burns (Plate 21): but in any case, we are informed that, alas, his love was not returned.

30 **A Triumvirate of Methodists: James Hamilton, John Wesley and Joseph Cole**
1790 2/56

This was sketched during Wesley's last visit to Scotland. In fact, Kay got his facts wrong: the famous preacher was a mere 87 at the time.

31 **Two travellers, James Bruce and Peter Williamson**
1791 1/59

Kay actually saw these two travellers meet at the Cross of Edinburgh, and stand in the street talking – though we may doubt whether the words of his caption were actually spoken. Bruce, the discoverer of the source of the Nile, met with a good deal of disbelief in the more extraordinary parts of his narrative, though subsequent travellers vouched for every word of it. Peter Williamson, when he came to publish his adventures, similarly found it hard to get his true account accepted. He had been kidnapped and sold as a slave in the United States. He won his freedom, only to be taken captive by Indians. Ultimately and almost miraculously he escaped, returned to Britain, published his story in which he named those responsible for his kidnapping – only to have it destroyed as a libel, and to be himself banished as a vagrant. Eventually right triumphed: he started a business on the base of his remuneration, became a publisher and as such issued the first Street Directory in Edinburgh and established the first Penny Post in Scotland.

32 **A Highland Chieftain: George, Fifth Duke of Gordon**
1791 1/78

Depicted while the Duke, then Marquis of Huntly, was serving with the 42nd Regiment at Edinburgh Castle. He later raised the Gordon Highlanders.

33 **Sir John Sinclair, statesman**
1791 2/23

Sinclair was the author of *The Statistical Account of Scotland.*

34 **The Evening Walk: Captain James Justice and a lady**
1792 1/130

The lady, though known to Kay's annotator, is discreetly not named. The Captain was not the best of husbands, and is reported as having greeted a visitor at his house thus: 'O, know your father well – not at all like him; no doubt of your mother – but – pshaw! – never mind. Welcome to Bachelor's Hall: 'tis Bachelor's Hall now, you know – Mrs Justice has left me – no matter – she was a good sort of person for all that – a little hot tempered – only three days after marriage, a leg of mutton made to fly at my head; never mind – plenty of wine, eggs, at Bachelor's Hall – we can make ourselves merry.' It is almost impossible not to suspect Dickens of having had a hand in the script.

35 **Thomas Blair, Deputy-Comptroller of the Stamp Office**
1792 1/142

36 **Henry Dundas and Sir James Stirling**
1792 1/150

During a period of high political feeling, the Home Secretary, Henry Dundas (later Lord Melville) made himself very unpopular by certain measures, and Provost Stirling who had to implement them was in considerable danger during the riots in Edinburgh city. Kay shows him sheltering under Dundas' coat till the danger shall be over.

37 **Captain Billair and his wife**
1792 2/129

Captain Richard Billair was chiefly noted for the tallness of his wife who actually went so far as to accentuate the fact by wearing high-heeled shoes – and, according to Kay's print, pattens and a tall hat into the bargain.

38 **Mr and Mrs Lee Lewes in The Road to Ruin**
1792 2/87

39 **Mary Queen of Scots**
1793 Sup/4

This print was made for Robertson's *History of Scotland*. Though it is of course not an original portrait, it shows how good an illustrator Kay was compared with the average eighteenth-century hack.

40 **The Rev James Lapslie, Minister of Campsie**
1793 2/39

This is an attack on a Minister who played a somewhat unethical role in the notorious Thomas Muir treason case. He is depicted as reading his own Essay on the Management of Bees, who can be taken as symbolising the cloud of witnesses to his shabby conduct. Though this is one of Kay's few positively hostile prints, it nevertheless lacks the virulence and savagery of most contemporary political satire – and was probably all the more effective through being insidiously witty rather than openly vindictive.

41 **Archibald Gilchrist, an Edinburgh Volunteer**
1794 1/98

The Prince of Wales' coronet is there to signify that, when not engaged in his military pursuits, Mr Gilchrist was a fashionable haberdasher who proudly boasted the princely warrant.

42 **Colonel Patrick Crichton of the Edinburgh Volunteers, with a view of the Awkward Squad**
1794 1/155

43 **James, Third Earl of Hopetoun, with the Hopetoun Fencibles**
1795 1/81

44 **Ensign Macdougal of the Hopetoun Fencibles**
1795 1/166

This young officer had so juvenile an appearance that the boys used to cry as he passed, 'There goes the Sucking Officer!' He survived such ordeals to grow to reach 2 metres in height and well-proportioned with it, and to be reputed one of the most handsome men in the service.

45 **William Grinly, merchant and ship-broker: the Leith Volunteer**
1795 2/26

One of Kay's most astonishing *tours de force*. The bird simply signifies his subject's nickname of 'The Spread Eagle', but the manner of the juxtaposition is worthy of le douanier Rousseau.

46 **Petticoat Government: or, The Grey Mare is the Better Horse**
1795 2/78

A satire on Lord and Lady Breadalbane, the cause of which is unknown. Certainly the history of the couple is one of unusual mutual affection, so the question is hardly one of matrimonial incompatibility.

47 **Ensign Charles Johnstone of the Hopetoun Fencibles**
1796 2/76

This fine-looking officer was in fact only 15 years old at the time, but made up in enthusiasm what he lacked in years.

48 **Henry Johnston as Hamlet**
1795 2/106

Johnston enjoyed a brief period of fame when he was known, in the best eighteenth-century fashion, as 'the Edinburgh Roscius'. Unfortunately his career declined after his wife left him. The dropped stocking can be read as part of the Hamlet role or as a reflection on the actor.

49 **A military promenade**
1795 2/110

A group of portraits showing a typical Edinburgh sight during the warlike era of the Volunteers. The officer sporting a veil is Captain Hay, an eccentric who liked peering into lady's faces – which he had to do to see them, being short-sighted. Whenever a lady lowered her own veil at his approach, he would lower his own, muttering:

> 'I know what you mean,
> I'm too ugly to be seen!'

50 **Mrs Luckie Smith**
1795 2/145

Kay himself tells us that when Mrs Smith heard he planned to do a picture of her, 'she sent for him to come and get a proper look at her; but he did not choose to accept the invitation.' He does not tell us why not – she looks as though it would have been a rewarding occasion. But certainly from an artistic viewpoint it was unnecessary: the print was regarded by all as an excellent likeness, and is certainly one of Kay's most memorable productions.

51 **William Ramsay, Lord Panmure**
1795 2/146

52 **Dr Henry Moyes, lecturer on Chemistry**
1796 1/75

This was an age when science was regarded as a proper subject for all men and women who liked to think of themselves as well-informed. Though blind, Moyes' scientific knowledge was wide, and his lectures were well attended by the citizens of Edinburgh.

53 **Lord Adam Gordon, Commander of the Forces in Scotland**
1796 1/88

Lord Gordon died five years later from drinking lemonade when over-heated – one in the eye for the advocates of temperance.

54 **James M'Kean on trial for the murder of Buchanan the Lanark carrier**
1796 2/123

One of the interesting aspects of Kay's art is that he frequently chooses popular subject-matter which would be disdained by the 'real' artist. Here, in a field normally left to the popular wood-engraver for the street-ballad market, Kay demonstrates his skill to the full: the effect of the finely drawn foreground figures against the lightly-drawn background crowd is a superb achievement, yet executed so naturally and easily that one forgets how rarely one has ever seen the like.

55 **Major-General Alexander Mackay, Deputy Adjutant-General to the Forces in Scotland**
1796 2/6

56 **A Political Set-To; or 'Freedom of Election' illustrated**
1796 2/137

Kingham, the ferry town across the Firth of Forth from Edinburgh, was notorious for its riotous electioneering. Kay's plate depicts an actual incident, so complex in its origins and development that it requires ten pages of closely printed notes in Paton's collection. We include it as one of the artist's rare attempts to go beyond his customary field of portraiture – proving how right he was to stick to what he was best at: though agreeably clear and fresh in its treatment, this print hardly shows Kay up to his usual form.

57 **Modern nursing**
1796 Sup/13

This is intended as a satire on the short-waisted gowns of the period – and on the obstacles raised in the way of a hungry un-weaned infant!

58 **Admiral Duncan at the battle of Camperdown**
1797 1/146

This picture of the victorious Admiral on the quarter-deck of the *Venerable* makes a refreshing change from the usual pompous naval portrait.

59 **Sergeant-Major Patrick Gould of the 1st Regiment of Edinburgh Volunteers**
1797 2/15

'His manner to a pupil was somewhat abrupt, and his language not remarkable for its refinement,' Kay's annotator tells us. Someone once asked Gould, 'Pray, who is that you are drilling in the Print done by Kay?' The answer was highly characteristic – 'I can't say, sir, unless you turn him to the right-about-face.'

60 **John Adams, Master of the Royal Riding Menage**
1797 1/161

61 **Copperbottom's Retreat: William Forbes of Callendar**
1797 2/37

This shrewd gentleman made a fortune by cornering the copper market after getting private word that the British Navy planned to sheathe all their ships' bottoms in that metal. With some of the proceeds he bought the big house at Falkirk, which annoyed the locals: fearing an attack by the town mob, he ran away from his house one night, and looking back, mistook the glare of the town's iron-works for the firing of his own home. He probably did not think this print was at all funny.

62 **The Great and the Small: Major-General Roger Aytoun and the duc d'Angouleme**
1797 2/70

Kay beautifully conveys the contrast between the burly (1.92 m) Scotsman and the fragile emigré son of the future Charles X, who had escaped from Revolutionary France to Scotland. The 'aristocratic' expression on the duc's face is achieved with almost unbelievable economy and no indication of effort or contrivance.

63 **James Marshall, writer to the Signet**
1798 1/111

64 **Sir James Grant of Grant, with a view of the Strathspey (or Grant) Fencibles**
1798 1/113

65 **The Rev Rowland Hill preaching on the Calton Hill**
1798 1/135

When this popular preacher came to Edinburgh, so many wanted to hear him that no church could contain them: so he preached to congregations of 10 to 20,000 on the Calton Hill – as one amazed townswoman observed, 'Even the vera sodgers are gaun to hear the preachin!' As might be expected, the Establishment did not care for such enthusiasm, and the General Assembly did their best to warn the faithful against Hill: quite in vain, of course.

66 **General James Grant of Ballindalloch**
1798 2/8

It is not surprising to learn that this capable soldier was particularly fond of food, to the degree that he took his cooks with him on his campaigning. He lived, fat but healthy, to the age of 86.

67 **James Macrae, the fortunate Duellist**
1799 1/13

Macrae was said to practise his shooting on a barber's block, as the ex-barber artist shows us in his inset, wittily signing it 'Barber' for the benefit of his knowing customers. The practice paid off, and Macrae killed his man: but had to flee to France in consequence, and spent the remainder of his life abroad.

68 **Margaret Suttie, a salt hawker**
1799 2/59

Salt hawking was a trade which flourished during the era when salt was taxed: it came to an end when the tax was abolished. For some reason, salt hawkers were always women.

69 **Lieutenant-General Vyse, in command of the Forces in Scotland**
1800 2/116

70 **Tom Paine, author of 'The Rights of Man'**
1801 2/64

This plate was etched by Kay from a miniature sent from America.

71 **Neil Fergusson, advocate, and Joseph Borulawski, the little Polish Count**
1802 1/133

Borulawski had, at any rate according to his own account, a highly romantic life. Although an aristocrat, he was under the necessity of making a living; and found no better way of doing this than by exhibiting himself. But the idea of vulgar display was naturally repugnant to him, so he professed merely to 'receive company', giving a breakfast to which any member of the public might come, at a charge of 3*s* 6*d*. 'After undergoing the annoyance of "receiving company", he used to spend the evenings with those families who were kind enough to receive him into their domestic circle, where he always proved, if not a *great* addition, at least a very pleasing one.'

72 **Robert Macgachen, accountant of Excise**
1802 2/155

The reason for the caption is unknown, but not hard to guess.

73 **Toussaint l'Ouverture**
1802 Sup/8

Had l'Ouverture been a rebel against British dominion, he would doubtless have been execrated as a trouble-maker; but since it was against the French that the dictator of Haiti was rebelling, he became a popular hero in Britain, and as such Kay hailed him in this fine print.

74 **Dead game**
1802 Sup/22

Another unusual subject for Kay, and a fine piece of etching by any standards. The artist's favourite cat is one of the interested parties: if it was indeed the same cat that he had depicted in his self-portrait 16 years previously, it certainly added a long active life to its other attributes.

75 **O'Brien, the Irish giant**
1803 2/40

The caption is over-generous: O'Brien was in fact a mere 8 ft 1 in (2.70 m). But the scene depicted was an actual one: the visiting Irishman, finding Edinburgh rather too cold for comfort, ordered a greatcoat – an event which naturally excited general interest. The tailor never revealed how the measurements were made: Kay's print was perhaps intended as a hypothetical explanation to satisfy popular curiosity.

76 **Alexander M'Kellar, the Cock of the Green**
1803 2/72

M'Kellar was a golfer who carried his enthusiasm for the game to fanatical lengths. He would spend whole days on the Burntsfield Links, and even play the shorter holes by lamplight. His wife, in classic manner, disapproved. One evening she tried to shame him by bringing his dinner and nightcap to the Links. 'Apparently without feeling the wit of the satire, he good-naturedly observed that she might wait, if she chose, till the game was decided, for at present he had no time for dinner.'

77 **William Macdonald, officer to the Highland Society**
1803 2/114

78 **Paul I, Czar of Russia**
1804 Sup/3

Taken from an original drawing by a Russian who had been banished to Siberia for daring to portray the Imperial Autocrat in all his ugliness.

79 **The Honourable Francis William Grant of Grant, Colonel of the Inverness-shire Militia**
1804 2/148

80 **John Tait, the broom-maker**
1805 2/50

81 **The Witch of Endor**
1805 Sup/23

After Fuseli.

82 **John Steele, aged 109**
1805 2/126

A noted Perthshire beggar, as famous for his great strength as for his great age.

83 **The last sitting of the old Court of Session**
1808 2/130

This was the last sitting before the Court of Session was separated into two divisions. The Senators portrayed are, reading round the table from left to right, Lords Hermand, Balmuto, Bannatyne, Armadale, Cullen, Polkemmet, Hope, Sir Ilay Campbell, Dunsinnan, Craig, Glenlee, Meadowbank senior, Woodhouselee, Robertson and Newton. Kay has been criticised for his lack of sense of perspective: but clearly this case at least is a studied effect, in which perspective has been deliberately discarded with superb indifference. The result is a fresh, vivid image where going by the rule-book would have produced at best a piece of documentation.

84 **Archibald M'Arthur, Piper to Ranald Macdonald of Staffa**
1810 2/101

M'Arthur visited Edinburgh in 1810 in the retinue of his Chief, and took part in the annual Pipers' competition. Failing to carry off the first prize, he refused to accept the second, thus disqualifying himself from taking part in the event again.

85 **John Knox, the Reformer**
1810 Sup/5

This was taken from an original painting, and intended for an edition of Knox's works. As with the Mary Queen of Scots portrait, it is a vivid illustration of the new freshness Kay brought to everything he did, even when it was only a matter of working over some other artist's original.

86 **Hugh Macpherson, clerk to the Perth carriers**
1810 2/105

87 **Twelve Advocates**
1811 2/156

This collection is noteworthy for the inclusion, second from the top on the left, of Sir Walter Scott, already known as a poet but not yet as a novelist; and of Francis Jeffrey, fourth down in the same column.

88 **An Edinburgh Oyster Lass**
1812 2/113

Kay's annotator tells us: 'Stout, clean and blooming, if they are not the most handsome or comely of Eve's daughters, the goodly fish-dames of Modern Athens are at least the most perfect pictures of robust and vigorous health; and not a few of them, under the pea-jacket and superabundance of petticoat with which they load themselves, conceal a symmetry of form that might excite the envy of a Duchess.'

89 **M de Latour, the French painter**
1813 2/63

No explanation is forthcoming for this unusual choice of subject. Our own guess is that Kay, fond as he was of his own cat, had heard that Latour shared the same fondness. The similarity with his own self-portrait can hardly be mere coincidence.

90 **Robert Craig of Riccarton, seated at the door of his own house in Princes Street**
1815 2/108

We are told that Robert Craig was particularly fond of the open air. Here, aged 85, he is shown as too old to take much exercise – but still getting what fresh air he could.

91 **William Wilson, known as 'Mortar Willie', aged 107**
1815 2/35

This, probably Kay's finest portrait, shows us Mortar Willie still actively working as a chemist's assistant though more than 100 years old. He died as the result of a fall, while still in good health.

92 **Sergeant William Duff of the Black Watch**
1816 2/91

93 **Francis Jeffrey, lawyer, statesman and critic**
1816 2/132

94 **Isobel, widow of Francis Ellis, aged 105**
1816 2/53

Taken from a painting by William Donaldson. The old lady survived her shoemaker husband by 72 years.

95 **Three Social Friends: Robert Kay, Louis Cauvin and David Scott**
1817 2/144

Robert Kay was no relative of the artist.

96 **Archibald Campbell, City Officer**
circa 1822, unfinished 2/159

This was the last etching that John Kay made. His annotator tells us that 'the venerable artist, then about eighty years of age, complimented several of his friends with impressions, as the farewell production of his pencil, at the same time apologising for its unfinished state'. It is based on a watercolour now in the Scottish National Portrait Gallery.

7

Bibliography and Iconography

Kay's work is still largely unexplored territory. We know that the material so far revealed is still less than half his known production, simply as regards his etchings alone: in addition, there must be dozens if not hundreds of miniatures by his hand, for it was by these that he made his living. Nor can we doubt that there are oil paintings of his to be found. It is our hope that this book will act as a spur, urging collectors public and private to look more closely at some of their overlooked material, and perhaps unearth more of Kay's work and bring it to public notice. The authors and publisher would be most grateful to learn of any such discoveries.

The primary source is the collection of some 360 etchings published after the artist's death by Hugh Paton of 27 Horse Wynd and later of Adam Square, Edinburgh. In May 1836 he issued a prospectus announcing that he had acquired a number of Kay's plates from Margaret, his widow: 'the copperplates are in excellent condition, some of them having scarcely ever been printed from.' He proposed to publish these in monthly parts at 2*s* 6*d* a part. He attracted well over 1,000 subscribers, including the Queen.

A Series of Original Portraits and Caricature Etchings by the late John Kay, Miniature Painter, Edinburgh, was accordingly published by Paton during the years 1837–1838. Today the work is normally found bound in two quarto volumes; Volume I contains i–xix, 1–430, i–vii pages and includes 170 plates: Volume II contains 1–472, i–xi, i–ii pages and includes 159 plates. Some editions contain at the end of the second volume an optional Appendix, containing 28 plates which were not strictly speaking original portraits. Some copies omit these plates, even though they include some of Kay's most interesting etchings.

The extremely copious notes for this edition have provided historians with a wealth of unique information about Kay's subjects and the society of his time. They were written by a man named James Paterson, who was employed by Paton at 15 shillings a week, later rising to 25 shillings, which he considered to be a very low rate of pay. In his *Autobiographical Reminiscences*, Paterson tells us: 'I used to select from the stitched copy of the whole portraits such as I thought most appropriate for the ensuing number; and after consulting Mr Paton as to the best parties to apply for information – either by letter or personally – I then set to work to glean from all the sources accessible.' He was helped to some extent by some notes prepared by Kay and an associate named Callender in 1792, when the artist himself had some idea of publishing a collection. Paterson's notes were edited by an advocate named James Maidment.

In 1842 a second edition was called for. It was identical in contents and type-setting, but added three additional plates to the Appendix. It was on smaller pages, being 8vo, which involved cropping some of the larger prints or folding them.

In 1877 a third edition was published by A & C Black, who had acquired the plates from Paton and had them retouched. It was issued in two quarto volumes. The text was identical. With typical lack of foresight, the publishers then destroyed the copperplates.

In 1885 a fourth edition, known as the *Popular Letterpress Edition*, was published in London by Hamilton, Adams and in Glasgow by Thomas D Morison, two volumes 8vo. This was intended chiefly for the historian and scholar, and the emphasis is on the text rather than on the plates which have been accurately described as 'very inadequate'.

The Paton volumes contain the vast bulk of Kay's known work. No other collection of his work has ever been published, though individual plates have frequently been used – often without acknowledgement – as illustrations to histories and the like.

Among individual pictures which have been located, the following are the most interesting. Nearly all of them are included in this book, and fuller details are supplied in the preceding section.

At the Scottish National Portrait Gallery, Edinburgh

Self-portrait in oils (our frontispiece; see note to (i)), (catalogue no 892).

Archibald Campbell, the Lord Provost's Man, watercolour (catalogue no 958).

The Parliament Close and Public Characters in its etching/aquatint form, which we reproduce as our endpapers (see note to (ii), (catalogue SPL 174/1, key SPL IV 737–1)).

They also possess a drawing of James Watt which has been attributed to Kay. They are doubtful, and in our opinion they are right to be doubtful; none the less there is a considerable similarity with some of the unpublished drawings in the Royal Scottish Academy collection (see below) so the attribution may be correct. Certainly Watt would have been a likely candidate for Kay's pencil.

At the Royal Scottish Academy, Edinburgh

They possess a most interesting folio volume containing a random collection of drawings and loose prints by John Kay, and one by his son William (which we reproduce as Plate xv). The most interesting item is the watercolour self-portrait which we reproduce as Plate iii, but the whole collection throws fascinating light on Kay's methods. The majority of the contents are not identified. They were stuck in the book either by Kay's widow or by Charles Kirkpatrick Sharpe, who purchased them from her and subsequently presented the volume to the Royal Scottish Academy. (Shelf no H.7.10.)

At the National Gallery of Scotland

The Department of Prints and Drawings possesses a watercolour of *A Fireman and Linkboy*, which we reproduce as Plate vii. They also have a certain number of his other prints.

At the Huntly House Museum, Edinburgh

They possess the oil original of the view of Parliament Close. Full details are supplied in our notes.

At the Edinburgh Room, Edinburgh Public Libraries

They possess another copy of the Parliament Close picture in its engraved form, together with a curious early state of this print, described in our notes.

They also have the curious print of *The City Guard* which we reproduce as Plate xiv.

They have a copy of *The life and character of Robert Watt; who was executed for high treason at Edinburgh, the 15th October, 1794.* The book, which was published in 1795, contains a characteristic portrait frontispiece by Kay, which is not included in Paton's collection.

They also have a beautifully neat collection of newspaper cuttings etc. relating to Kay. These are of little original value in themselves, but are interesting as showing the kind of interest Kay has received over the last 100 years.

At the British Museum, London (Department of Prints and Drawings)

They possess, besides Paton's book, 104 prints, unmounted in a folder (catalogue c5*) and 206 more, privately bound into an album (catalogue 298*a8). Most of these also appear in Paton's book, though they have the advantage of being for the most part fine early prints, crisper than in the published book. There are about 15 etchings which do not appear either in Paton's book or in the present work: they comprise portraits of no outstanding interest, several not identified.

At the Mary Evans Picture Library, London

They possess, in addition to Paton's book, a number of loose prints, some of which are not to be found elsewhere; the most interesting is the one we reproduce as Plate xii (of which the Royal Scottish Academy possesses an unfinished state).

They also possess an interesting album of Kay etchings compiled by an unidentified collector in 1789. It contains 113 early prints, several of which are not to be found elsewhere, or in different states. The annotations are interesting: for example, on the print we reproduce as Plate 3 the comment is bluntly: 'A stupid attempt to represent Mrs Siddons.'

GOLDSMITHS HALL
WELSH
DOUNIE
AULD Goldsmith
REID
watch Maker
J MILLER